THE TRANS MANUAL

Layman's Guide to Gender Theory

Robert Gagnon

Fair Use and Copyright Disclaimer

IMAGE DISCLAIMER

The cover image is an AI-generated illustration. The person depicted is fictional and does not represent any real individual, living or deceased. Any resemblance to actual persons is purely coincidental.

NO ENDORSEMENT OR PROFESSIONAL REPRESENTATION

The image and content of this book do not imply endorsement, approval, or representation by any medical professional, organization, or governing body. The depicted imagery is illustrative only.

GENERAL DISCLAIMER

This book is provided for informational and educational purposes only. It does not constitute medical, psychological, or legal advice. Readers should consult qualified professionals regarding any specific concerns.

Contents

A Case of Simple Observation

There have been many controversial arguments about people transitioning to another gender in the past few years. As of this writing hundreds of anti-transitioning laws have been introduced citing the protection of children as their cause. To be fair to both sides I've decided to list, define, and break down in simple terms the different aspects of this topic.

This subject is not nearly as simple as it seems on its surface. Medical theories, genetic anomalies, faith and belief systems, along with human rights have been called into question. Definitions as simple as what is a man or a woman, is it gender or birth sex? What exactly is the difference between sex and gender? For the longest time these terms were interchangeable. The average person would spend years learning the intricacies of genetics, medicine, or psychology to a proficient degree before tackling these questions. That leaves the common citizen with little choice but to search the net or listen to influencers and our leaders. After researching this subject from every angle for the last few years it became obvious that there was no reliable source that broke this subject down to something everyone could understand. Every publication is either an endorsement or a criticism of Gender theory.

Not everyone has the advantage of higher education, but that doesn't mean we shouldn't be informed about matters that concern the world we live in. This is a manual for the layman by a layman. Anything you find questionable in this publication feel free to research yourself. You will find that both views have been plainly represented from a strictly observational viewpoint.

Simple observations mean exactly that. Science is based on consistently repeating an experiment and observing the results for irregularities or the lack thereof. Repeating any experiment under strictly controlled conditions with a minimum of 20, or more times with the same result constitutes established fact. If the observer is biased and misconstrues the results, the data is considered tainted and invalid. Only when the experiment can be repeated by anyone or group with the same outcome can the results assume the title of established scientific fact.

Once again, this book is about simple observations. Once fact has been established, theories as to why this experiment has an established result can vary. Everyone processes and sees things differently. Reality for some people can vary from the reality of the majority or within a small group. Perception of simple facts can be distorted to suit the individuals' personal view of the world and their place in it. There is only one reality, one everyone can observe and confirm with their senses. To deny reality negates our ability to accept or affect the physical world around us. It is this denial or questioning of reality that will be logically analyzed in this manual through simple observation.

Everyone has an opinionated filter that affects how input of any information is remembered and recalled. It is much easier to recall a given point in time that has an emotion attached to it than a simple memory with no personal feelings involved. The greatest priority is given to the most significant moments of our lives which have the greatest emotional impact. The deeper and stronger the emotional bond, the more a memory affects your perception.

Perception is often an opinionated observation tainted with bias; it has no place in establishing fact. So, let's start with the established facts the vast majority agree on. This is biology 101. Human reproduction in nature requires two subjects to reproduce. One female and one male. The male has a penis, external scrotum that contains the testicles and a prostate to inject the semen from the testicles into the urethra. The semen contains the sperm that fertilizes the female egg. The female has ovaries that produce the female egg which travels through a fallopian tube to the womb.

During coitus the sperm then travels towards the egg and attempts to penetrate the egg wall. In a successful insemination, the sperm pierces the egg wall where DNA is shared between the two subjects. The resulting cells multiply into an embryo, form a fetus, and if everything goes well a new human being. If you are alive today, it is because of the reproductive properties of a man and a woman. It is cut and dry what the human reproductive facts are in the real world.

Disorders of sexual development (DSDs) are an exception. Sometimes there are mistakes in nature. An individual may have characteristics of both sexes, or no genitalia at all. Internal testicles in a person with a woman's fully functional reproductive system, or a functional male with visible or internal female reproductive parts. These cases have historically been treated as birth defects and are often treated soon after birth with surgical intervention. With function used as a guide, the least dominant or nonfunctional genitalia would be removed. In this way a child could grow up appearing and functioning as a normal male or female. Without the trauma of being different and less medical complications.

In recent years there have been debates concerning infants' rights to make their own decision as to what sex they may want to go through life as. But at what age should this decision be made? What about the years of suffering and self-doubt that comes with being different from everybody else. What to do in a case where (although rare) both male and female genitalia are potentially functional. A documentary by intersex people titled "Intersexion" is very informative on this subject. In this documentary intersex adults felt cheated out of their choice. It addresses how their parents were instructed to treat their birth as something to be ashamed of, including moving to a new city where no one would know about the surgical correction of the child.

Newborn surgical intervention to correct intersex is a decision for parents to make under a doctor's supervision. Although these decisions should never be made hastily or with only one doctor's opinion, parents can gain a better grasp on what is in a child's best interests. In the event that atypical genitalia impede normal bodily functions surgery may be necessary. Each case will vary as to what the best medical solution may be, including no surgical intervention at all. In the United Kingdom non-emergency intersex operations must go before a review board first. This board strongly leans away from surgical intervention in infants, preferring to leave the decision up to the patient during or post puberty.

We can now state the fact that nature has established the roles of the human male and female in terms of reproduction. There is no question as to what makes a man or a woman, it is determined at birth by genitalia, with few exceptions. Birth defects do not designate a different sexual category, nor does it place the binary concept on any imaginary spectrum. In terms of reproduction a male and female are required to produce offspring in nature. Intersex is identified as having both of the binary characteristics. Recently the AMA has suggested removing sex as a designation from birth certificates. The reason being that it discriminates against individuals by separating them into two different categories according to genitalia and reproductive purpose. This theory also addresses the previously mentioned people suffering from sexual ambiguity as being excluded from the binary system that has been in place from the dawn of mankind.

Why the AMA would endorse an ideology that is clearly contrary to the science of human anatomy may seem puzzling at first. Something has changed within the last few decades, to sway the medical community away from the facts. Every doctor knows the biological difference between men and women along with their individual needs. To nullify their binary differences serves no medical advantage. If anything, this type of thought muddies the waters pertaining to the optimal outcome of any medical intervention. Recent discoveries in different combinations of X and Y chromosomes, along with the various genital birth defects found in nature, are cited as a bellwether moment. Suddenly sex is not binary, but a variety of possibilities with as many variations as there are humans on the planet. This is the conclusion of an uninformed, atypical, or immature mind. Everyone is different, short, tall skinny or overweight, but they still fall into the binary category of male or female with very few anomalies. Nothing has changed in terms of human reproduction; it takes one of each sex to reproduce in nature. Any other conclusion is an obtuse opinion not based on fact.

Humans have found other uses for their genitalia besides reproduction. Sexual pleasure being the most prominent. Whether through manual self-stimulation or with another person, the human orgasm is about the most intense form of physical pleasure the human body can experience. Combined with emotions such as love, desire, or anticipation, this experience can be enhanced to even higher forms of gratification. In the pursuit of sexual pleasure, reproduction can become secondary or completely irrelevant. What attracts or excites sexual interest towards another person may negate the entire process of reproduction. These alternative possibilities will be discussed in the next chapter.

The Adult Playground

Human sexuality can take on unlimited forms and variations. Engaging in sex for pleasure can be quite satisfying and in some cases addictive. A common term when referring to sex is the adult playground, where consenting adults can learn, practice, or just experience different sensations with someone else. Having an open mind and consideration along with respect for your sexual partner/s needs can go a long way in reciprocal forms of pleasure. What each person is attracted to is particular to each individual. Some are attracted to intelligence, physical appearance, humor, financial or physical strength to name a few. There is also the matter of sexual preference. This involves same sex, opposite sex, and either sex. Let's break down these three categories of sexual preference so everyone can be on the same page.

Latin is a dead language meaning that it cannot change or evolve to mean anything other than a blunt description. It has been used for legal and medical terms for just this reason. It cannot be mistranslated in any questionable form. This has been the primary language used for legal and medical terms for centuries. I will refer to Latin terminology for the same specific descriptions that a doctor would use in most instances.

All nonextinct humans that currently inhabit the earth are known as homo sapiens. Homo is the genus or group that are referred to as man and sapiens from the Latin word for wise. A homosexual is a man that is attracted to and/or engages in sex with another man. Regardless of gender it takes two men, born as men to engage in homosexual activity. They can both be masculine, feminine or exchange and mix roles. Gender refers to masculine or feminine traits or roles in a traditional male and female relationship. No matter how either one of the participants in a homosexual exchange of activity may view themselves, it is still homosexual activity. The preferred phrase most homosexuals prefer is Gay. It sounds more appealing than the Latin alternative.

Homosexuality is not limited to men. Women that are attracted to or engage in sexual activity with other women are known as Lesbians. This term comes from the Greek island Lesbos. The term was first used in English literature when referring to the writings of Saffo, a female poet known for her exceptional ability to express her feelings in ancient Greece 6th century BC. Lesbos was where she spent most of her life and forever left her mark for the literary world. Lesbians can be feminine, masculine, or any degree in between. The more masculine are sometimes referred to as butch and the more feminine as femme. These are a couple of common labels loosely used to describe sexual or gender roles, and not necessarily any form of identification. Although some Lesbians may go out of their way to embellish an appearance of masculinity, there are no set expectations in a lesbian relationship, other than self-imposed ones.

Bisexuality comes from the Latin binarius meaning two. Bi is used in English as a prefix in such words as bicycle or bipedal. In the case of bisexuals, it refers to a person that sexually interacts with or is attracted to both sexes. A male or female bisexual can engage with either sex or both simultaneously, with no limitation to any degree of ratio from the same or the opposite sex. Bisexuals reportedly make up more than half of the LGB community. Granting them the lion's share of membership while leaving the gay and lesbian members to split the rest. It has been a personal observation from conversations with members of the LGB community throughout the years that a pure gay or lesbian individual are somewhat rare.

By purity I mean that they have never experienced any sexual activity with the opposite sex. In the 90's I had the opportunity to associate with a group of about 30 Lesbians for over a year. The common element was trust. Most of these women had bad experiences with men. Sometimes with family members, straight relationships, molestations, or betrayals of friends because of their lifestyle. The list of reasons is extensive. One thing they all agreed on, only one of their group never had sex with a man. She was referred to as "the real thing" and was held in high regard almost reverence.

The gay guys I've met over the years weren't so complicated. After all guys are guys, and we can all communicate at some level. Gays tend to be social and extraverted when comfortable with their surroundings. Most of them are not weighed down with the expense of children or ex's, which leaves more for self-indulgence. Hard working, usually educated, and well informed, I've really enjoyed conversation with most of these guys. I could never construct a ratio of pure gays because it held no relevance to them. Gay men seem to value friendship and acceptance above an "us or them" mentality.

Most gay men I have known had tried sex with women while still identifying as exclusively gay. Their common opinion was, that they had tried sex with women and found the experience less satisfying. The conclusion to these observations is that people prefer what they like but may also remain open to other possibilities. This is a reasonable conclusion that applies to most people.

Bisexuals will have sexual relations with or attraction to the same or opposite sex. Though most tend to have a preference and wander towards the alternative when the situation suits them. Bisexuals can be in a monogamous relationship with either sex for any length of time or more on the promiscuous side. To be physically Bi infers multiple sex partners, though one or more of those partners may be more of a relationship.

Open marriages, relationships, and swinging suit many couples whether straight or LGB. Though bringing one or more outsiders into a binary relationship may strain the relationship, some couple's approach polygamy as a team sport. Bisexuals have the largest selection of mates to pick from, since their preferences encompass anyone that will couple with them.

Every human being feels the need to belong to something greater than themselves. This need is met at many different levels in the form of friends, family, groups, or other various types of relationships. Humans tend to be social creatures that seek out others that are more like themselves than different. Social structures can form with as few as three people. The two most alike will form a bond, while the third person will commonly have the lesser say on matters of agreement. Children learn this at a very young age, when picking teams for play or basic interaction. In terms of team sports the most effective players are chosen first, the most popular or well-liked of the average players next, leaving the least able and unpopular for the latter. Ability usually overrides popularity unless the captain picking the team wants to ensure a close friend makes it on his team to prevent friction from that same friend later.

This same pecking order can be seen in any social situation, from work environment, school, and amongst siblings. It is an instinctive pattern of behavior emanating from the need to compete for limited resources. These resources can be material or emotional, including the need to dominate others for control over anything of value. By the same token, no human communicates with another without something to gain. This could be for mutual interest, information, companionship, curiosity or out of boredom to occupy time until someone better comes along. There is no reason to speak without some form of goal to be achieved, sometimes just to hear one's own voice fulfils the need for self-aggrandizement and validation.

When parents instruct, or teach their children, the goal is safety, improvement of life, or assimilation into the family dynamic. Outside of parental influence our interactions may expose us to others that may not have our best interest in mind. Whenever two or more people meet, they usually make a brief visual assessment before a verbal greeting. If that goes well, a soft question or compliment will usually follow to fish for likely responses. At this early stage, a decision is made whether there is anything to gain from getting to know this person. Information, entertainment, friendship, physical relations, or just basking in the glow of their personality, what do I gain? The more alert person may read another's body language and gauge that against past acquaintances. This would affect the opening conversation regarding being more open or guarded in the exchange of information. In the event a person in your orbit is perceived as a threat in any way, it may be best not to reveal much about yourself or personal opinions. There's no need to rock the boat in a social situation, unless you feel the need to express your opinion to an established opponent or ally.

What does any of this have to do with human sexuality? As everyone jockeys for their position in the social maze of human interaction, each individual must establish a sexual identity as well. One that best represents their feelings and beliefs in the sexual realm. One such realm, the LGB faction, has had it harder than most. Classified as a mental illness until the late sixties, they have been ostracized, imprisoned, and committed for their sexual attraction to their own kind. Many established religions promote their existence as a malicious plague on humankind. They are simply people with a certain sexual attraction that some may find unacceptable.

Let's admit that human sexuality has no boundaries. Any possible act between two or more people has and will be acted out by some seeking non-typical fulfilment. Why do so many think that a straight sadomasochistic relationship is more tolerable than a gay one? A straight male being degraded by a woman in leather seems to be more socially acceptable than gay marriage. The Hetero reasoning is that bazaar as S&M is, it's still between a man and a woman in this instance. The best term to describe this reaction is stigma. The word stigma will be discussed frequently in later chapters as it has been morphed to encompass other meanings. In most situations it means a bad reputation or having a historic negative connotation.

This brings us to a depravity, which everyone except the perpetrators agree is a crime against nature, pedophilia. This is when an adult contributes to the sexual corruption of a child.

Whether through direct sexual contact or suggestion, the desecration of a child's innocence is the worst betrayal of humankind.

It is a parent's responsibility to protect their children as best they can by teaching them what is and is not appropriate touching. Making responsible decisions about who the child can be left in care of or be exposed to. Make them aware of their bodies without shame of who they are and teach them to love themselves just as they are. Answer age-appropriate questions and find out what initiates questions they shouldn't be asking. They had to get it from somewhere.

Pedophiles come in all ages and can be male or female, straight, gay or bisexually oriented. Adolescents can prey on younger neighbors or relatives avoiding the scrutiny often applied to adults. There have been cases of high schoolers tricking other students into compromising videos then blackmailing them into prostitution. High tech predators use the internet in the same way, sometimes luring both younger and older children from their home, for sexual abuse or possible sale to others.

There has been one very open organization of these child molesters called NAMBLA, the North American Man Boy Love Association. Co-founded in 1978 by Gay rights activist David Thorstad. They not only endorse adults having sex with children toddler age to fifteen, they also went to court to legalize it. In 1993 the International Lesbian and Gay Association (ILGA) reached consultive status with the U.N. but fell under scrutiny for including NAMBLA in their organization. ILGA did drop NAMBLA, and another organization, from their roster but were themselves also dropped from the U.N. in 1994 for dragging their feet on

NAMBLAs expulsion. It was 2006 before ILGA was allowed readmittance at the U.N. The vast majority of LGB members are as repulsed by pedophiles as straight people. But a small radical faction of pedophiles imbedded themselves into the LGB movement and tried promoting a "united we stand" attitude toward NAMBLA within the LGB community. This has given the LGB community a bad reputation for sexual matters concerning children. The stigma from this association has remained to this day.

Most NAMBLA members have gone underground, working the dark web, or managing the seedy sex trafficking rings sometimes mentioned in the news. The more public ones argue in the courts to this day that all convicted child molesters should be released from jail. They claim that molesters cannot help themselves and were just born that way. Some have expressed that the term "child molester" has a stigma attached to it, and that Youth Attracted Persons is the preferred term to use. As if whitewashing their description legitimizes their perversion. The vast majority of the LGB community recognize child molesters as the criminals they are and should not be associated with these predators because of their personal adult sexual preference.

We can now safely conclude that reproductive sex is binary. Sexual attraction or encounters with others can be straight, gay, lesbian or bisexual. No labels or Initials anyone may try to apply changes this basic fact. There are no gray areas between these sexual preference descriptions as to function. No opinion or point of view has any effect on this fact. There are only the two sexes, one sperm producing male and one egg producing female for sexual reproduction in nature. Sex organs serve only one purpose in nature, reproduction. What the individual does with their body parts is a personal decision. This is verified by simple observation.

The Id

Humans are social creatures and as such require other humans to interact with for multiple reasons, the most imperative being survival. From birth a sense of family develops that comes from parent to child. Comfort and feeding are the first interactive experiences after birth. The repetition of discomfort and hunger when alone, then appeasement of these needs with another's contact makes necessity of contact with others more instinctive. Next observation of the infant would be the cooperation between more than one parent or parent and other siblings. This sense of family and belonging form an ingrained reliance on the company of others for growth through interaction. Learning, communication, and developing skills for survival all stem from this social reliance.

Every family has its own dynamic that a child learns through observation during interaction with others at home. Sometimes these lessons interphase simultaneously with other influences from outside the family unit. Whether it happens in a daycare, or a village situation, infants and toddlers primarily lean towards family for their needed sense of belonging. At the end of any journey, however small or large, the young individual is always returned to the family they know and adhere to. This instils a sense of security and belonging, a familiarity they are a part of.

In our current observations I will be referring to a nominal person with full faculties. The first true sense of self comes from possession. Repetition of the name an infant is known by creates an identity. This identity belongs to that individual alone, along with this new individuality comes possessions. Favorite toys, blanket, and bottles form the comfort system to support and represent the individual. Words are taking on meaning, more so how they are said as much as what is said. "No" and "Bad" are accompanied with a negative connotation as compared to a positive for "yes" and "good". Mobility usually occurs in the young individual before articulate speech. Crawling leads to exploring all the things observed but previously out of reach. During the early process of exploration different items are expressed as possessions of others or community property. Concepts of what's yours, what's mine or ours develop along with what is dangerous or safe. These base concepts shape the view of every identifiable item committed to memory.

As objects are identified and assimilated, so are concepts of self. With exposure to siblings, other children and adults, the binary concept of sex and gender are observed. Male and female dress, sound and act differently in a normal traditional environment. By 18-24 months an infant can well distinguish between the two for themselves. Along with observations, the terms boy or girl including the correct pronouns her, him, he, she, his, hers are applied repeatedly to the child. This instills a sense of self and where the child fits in with the binary concept of sexual identity. An observant parent will reinforce these norms if their child becomes confused as to which group they belong to. This is known as traditional positive reinforcement. Girls are pretty or beautiful while boys are good looking or handsome, this is a common traditional example of positive role reinforcement.

Identity by sex can never be altered but, misalignment of gender and sex can occur through neglect or simple accident.

Children with mental deficiencies, emotional or learning issues are more easily confused by the binary concept. With patience, any child can be taught to be proud of who and what they are. Any delusion that they can physically change what they are should never be allowed or encouraged to grow without intervention. If these thoughts are left unchecked, they subconsciously lend validity to the concept that the child's sex at birth is a mistake and has no true value. This leads to the deep-seated self-assumption that the individual as a whole is a mistake with no or lesser value.

A modern theory that has gained popularity with gender theorists is authenticity. This movement believes that society has corrupted the adult mind to conform to norms enforced by society. Conformity to societal norms is the basis for any civil interaction among a given group. As with any group of people, some individuality must give way to the greater good of the majority. This does not mean that the individual disappears. It only implies that the nonconformity of one or a few individuals will not be prioritized over the will of the majority.

This is an unacceptable condition of human nature according to the authenticity crowd. They believe anything a child thinks or imagines should never be questioned or corrected as a child forms their sense of self. Gender theorists insist the concept of a binary gender should never be forced on any child since this may differ from the child's own uninformed and unguided conclusions. Some parents go out of their way to avoid instructing a toddler to identify with the gender reflecting their sex. They claim the old parenting techniques have caused nothing but mental trauma through societal expectations. Despite the overwhelming proof that children raised by these traditional values are one fifth as likely to contemplate or commit suicide or self-harm during their lifetime.

This blatant lack of guidance is coming from the first generation to experience less direct parental interaction. Beginning with the internet and expanded by the distribution of smart phones, parents interact more with technology than with their own children. Leaving young minds to reach poor conclusions based on erroneous information. Then the "authentists" revel in how much they can learn from their children.

The concept that the child is wiser than the parent and instinctively knows what is best for them is blatantly false. Were it true, kids would live on candy, ice cream, hot dogs, and fast food. It is a lot more work to guide and nurture a child to become the best they can be, with a sense of self-worth, and pride in themselves. None of these positive results can be accomplished without a solid foundation built on facts and constructive examples. It is the competent parents' responsibility to establish these facts through example and conversation.

Humans tend to generalize everything in a binary term when referring to how we perceive the world. Hot or cold, far or near, right or wrong, etc. These are terms normally used to set parameters of two extremes. Everything between these markers is either dead center (average) or various degrees between the set goals. This is the same way adults describe any subject when communicating with each other. Children develop this same sense of scale as their vocabulary and vocal skills become more articulate.

At birth the child's brain is one fourth the size of an adult. Within twelve months brain size has doubled and has continued to develop neural pathways to interpret, store and organize everything the senses receive. Walking, balance, gross and some fine motor skills have developed along with some word recognition and limited speech. The growing brain has served its purpose as a sponge for soaking up and retaining information. But it will have to take a big leap in capacity and ability for the next part of human development.

Freud described the three stages of Human thought as Id, Ego, and Superego. Harris in 1972 referred to the same stages as child, parent, and adult. Both sets of terms describe the same phases of human development separated by a major shift in brain activity. The first of these two major shifts are marked by the rapid growth of neural pathways developing in the brain, between 18 and 24 months. At twelve months the brain has doubled in size and will grow to 90% of full size by the age of five. A process called neural pruning also begins to elevate at twelve months. Think of this process as a form of scan disc and formatting in the human brain. Weak, irregular, or infrequent electrical pathways are turned off or given less priority. Continuously used pathways are reinforced and added to like a series of rivers each with its own purpose. Think of one river for each of the senses, others for movement, speech, thought etc. These rivers of electrical connections grow more efficient and refined as they are added to. The pruning sorts the information and trims the turbulence while preventing any leakage or irregularities between them.

In this current development, speech will improve from 20 to about 50 words with some words linked together. Children can refer to themselves by name, know body parts and convey needs along with running, jumping, and sorting items by color or size. Screen time should be very limited during this phase, while encouraging as much interaction with others as possible. Reading from printed books while pointing at the words and explaining illustrations gives meaning and substance to words and images.

By 24 months your child should understand between 200 and 500 words and start to form some independence. Sitting on a couch in front of a TV stifles mental and physical development and should be limited during the child's waking hours. The more social interaction and productivity a child observes and takes part in, the more of the same will be exhibited in the child's behavior.

Social environment directly affects patterns of thought along with how information is processed. In a negative household environment, a child would tend to view the world in a more negative sense. The opposite could be said for a child in a positive environment. The radical element in this theory is trauma or an outside influence that can alter behavior throughout a person's lifetime. In early development, before speech is comprehended words are heard and stored. The parents may believe that there is no harm in saying something negative about a child in their presence. Although the full comprehension of the comment cannot be processed at that time, the words and tone are deeply embedded in the subconscious.

As comprehension of language grows, so does this imbedded seed. This seed along with the accumulation of others are what make up the core of every individual. Hearing that they are smart, strong, fearless, or independent becomes some of the child's view of self. Negative seeds such as needy, whiney, "this one was an accident", or "we really wanted a girl" can cause lifelong negative impressions of self, resulting in poor behavior, decisions, and outcomes.

Trauma can manifest itself in many forms. A small example is when the parent, as a very young child, tracked mud into the house. Their parent yells and physically punish them resulting in an intense fear response in the child. They do not remember the incident, but when their own child tracks mud in the house decades later an auto response takes over. This response will mimic or have an amplified result when the subconscious is triggered. The stronger the original trauma the more intense the response. Now amplify that single incident by the hundreds, and you have the core of most humans' psyche.

Not all emotional responses are bad. Love, compassion and empathy are just as strongly triggered when an individual witnesses similar situations. Auto responses are just as described, they are not thought out or contrived. Self-control is the only safety net that keeps most people from making drastic mistakes that could negatively affect their lives. Look before you leap or think before you jump can be a lifesaving idiom.

Children are a mirror of the world around them. Through observation and mimicry, they learn to interact with others in the same fashion they have observed. In a calm household where everyone is productive and conversations are conducted in a rationally organized format; the child will assume these same mannerisms. In a combative atmosphere, where arguing, yelling and physical altercations are the norm, a child will incorporate these same techniques in their interactions with others.

Exertion of their will using the word "no" or other forms of defiance such as manipulating control by throwing tantrums will be tested for effectiveness. If you allow these behaviors to persist or they become profitable for the child, they will rightly assume they have control. An observant parent will immediately curtail these behaviors using the punishment and reward system. It's called behavior modification; the parent must always exert control for everyone's benefit. The child must learn to exhibit and practice self-control. The parent should never punish a child out of anger. Only constructive punishments should be executed as well as deserved rewards.

Behavioral modification is also structural modification. Every child needs a template to follow to interact with others while maintaining a sense of self. Rules and guidelines must be taught and enforced in the early years along with lessons on empathy, such as understanding the thoughts and needs of others. Explain that you can't learn if you don't listen. Whenever children have doubts about facts or opinions learned outside the home, take the time to make a valuable lesson about the issue at hand. Children look towards an adult or older sibling as a responsible source of information while building their image of themselves and the world around them. If you let outside influences direct their self-image, you will lose their respect as a reliable source of information. This is where the familiar term "bad influences" originates from. Do not allow such seeds to take root in your child's psyche.

The Ego

The Ego or parent has already emerged from the first sense of self that an infant experiences. As the Id served its purpose to obtain sustenance and other basic needs through impulse, the Ego evolves to temper those drives. Think of the Id as our ferocious animalistic hunger for gratification. There is no right or wrong, only need accompanied by every untethered emotion. Once realization of self is established, the Id losses its' monopoly to the Ego, though by no means does it disappear. Now the Id has a new tool to feed it, a force of its own, not dependent on others. The adage "I think, therefore I am" takes on real meaning. The ego becomes the vehicle by which all things desired can be obtained.

From early on, reaching for, pointing and some vocalizations of glee or distress can manipulate others to deliver the desired items. Mobility adds to the availability of anything that catches an infant or toddlers' interest. Oral fixation (the pleasure food and drink bring) makes every object a potential prize that immediately gets tasted. The id will forever want and need to be satisfied but, it's the Ego that gets things done. Id becomes the subconscious, and Ego becomes the conscious thought process until the age of five when the Superego arrives.

The terrible twos are the next stage of development. This part of child development could best be described as the frustration phase. Lacking fine motor skills, and limited ability to fully express themselves children experience frustration which leads to tantrums. Additional elements could be hunger or fatigue. This period of development can range from 12 months to 4 years of age. Crying, screaming, hitting, throwing things are behaviors that although not uncommon must be addressed. Rewarding bad behavior sends the wrong message, that poor behavior comes with benefits. If communication or distraction has no effect the best response is to remove the item or situation from the equation. Once the tantrum has ended, explain that the behavior was inappropriate. Labeling the child as bad is not recommended, just insist the behavior was bad and that good children shouldn't do bad things.

Be wary of children that make a scene knowing they will get attention by acting up. Put them in time-out or sit with them and say how disappointed you are, but do not play into their manipulation. Once the incident is resolved don't dwell on their misbehavior, time is relative to age. An hour to a two-year-old is like a day to an adult. If tantrums progressively get worse or more frequent, it's time to discuss these behaviors with a pediatrician.

Imagination and fantasy play is very constructive in forming social development. From 18 months to the age of seven, imagination assists in language skills, interaction with others, empathy, and a never-ending range of possibilities. Every great invention comes from imagination, taking material things and combining them mentally to create something new. The more a child knows, the more complex their thought process becomes. Fantasy play alone or with other children allows them to work things out and discover new worlds and how they respond to them. Role play creates heroes and villains along with dialogue that can occupy hours of a child's day, while building concepts of boundaries and rules. Encouraging imagination is one of the greatest gifts you can give a child. Creativity is born in our imagination. If you are a creative adult, it originated from this time in your life. If not encouraged, it will begin to fade around age seven. If fantasy is constructive, and not an escape from reality there is no harm in keeping a healthy imagination throughout your lifetime. After all, imagination is the mother of invention, art, math and literature.

Superego

At age five the brain has reached 90 percent of its potential growth. Most children at this age can't differentiate between belief and knowing something, the contrast in physical reality and perception, or how to interpret the difference. Now the final part of the psyche comes into play, the Superego or Adult. The Adult completes the human thought process by balancing everything the individual has learned and experienced. It is our internalized acceptance of rules and morals learned from parents, friends and the observed behavior of others.

When the Id wants something, the Ego forms the plan to obtain it, the Adult weighs the pros and cons of what approach is acceptable to fulfil the Ids desire. Say a 6-year-old sees a red bike, he (the Id) really wants it, the Ego says we can take it, the Superego says stealing is wrong, let's ask Mom for one and see how that works out. The Adult works as a safety valve of checks and balances, using concepts of right and wrong, good or bad and the difference between could and should. It is our conscious decision maker and our conscience tempered by the Ego. Superego can best be defined as our personality. Although the elements of Id and Ego hold sway towards our behavior, it is the Superego that finalizes how we treat and communicate with others.

In a perfect world, every individual's psyche would develop the same way with no trauma or obsessive behavior. In the real world, everything we have ever experienced or learned combines to form our individual personalities. The most notable of these experiences are traumas. Anything witnessed or experienced that shocks the psyche leaves an impression like a snapshot in time. These moments in time act like filters or amplifiers that can affect anything from the occasional thought to every waking moment of our life.

A simple example would be a very loving and calm parent becoming loud and aggressive when a young child is about to touch something very hot. Yelling "don't touch that!" startles the child creating an auto response that will in this case benefit the individual's safety throughout their lifetime. An intensely fearful response may result in a lifetime of avoiding any experience that an individual may perceive as being a similar threat.

The ID being the source of all emotional drives is also the source of our fears. Once an incident triggers the Ids flight mode, any similar situation real or imagined can become a source of extreme anxiety. Any part of the body can be the focus of this anxious response. Persistent hand washing, hair grooming, anorexia are all results of a run-away ID response.

I once knew a woman in her twenties that always said "dirty stinky feet" instead of simply feet. Someone at an influential time in her life made that statement and left an imprint that remains to this day. In the same way, some people may focus and stress over genitalia. Both sexes urinate from their genitalia and are taught when young that this area must be kept clean. This can easily be misinterpreted in a young mind as a dirty part of the body with a negative connotation. Repetition of special attention brought to this area may ensure cleanliness, but it also prioritizes importance. Being reassured at an early age that every part of the body requires attention, and that there are no bad parts can contribute to a less stressful life. While for some, a fixation with their genitals can manifest itself in many negative ways.

Since reproductive sex is binary, humanity has been divided into two base identities of male and female. In nature only females can give birth and feed a baby with their bodies. The male is only required to inseminate the female in the initial part of the reproductive process. If a male expects to see their progeny prosper and grow, they contribute to the female and child's well-being. This is where the concept of gender originated.

Different behaviors are evident between the sexes in all mammals. The females and young are almost always protected by the males in a family, pack or tribal unit. Perpetuation of the species requires more emphasis on the safety of the females and offspring than the males. As an example, when the Titanic was sinking, the limited lifeboats were filled with women and children first. The more women and children that survive the greater our chances as a species. It would require only a few males to insure genetic variety.

The more expendable males are left to compete for the limited resources available. Testosterone creates greater muscle mass, strength and aggressiveness, in males. This has led to their more assertive and dominant predisposition. Physical strength and competitive spirit have traditionally been encouraged and admired more so in men than women. Competition between women can be just as fierce as competition between men when it comes to resources. In a misogynous society (which most are) males with the most appeal, resources or power are highly sought after and battled over by females. Not only to elevate their own station but to secure a better future for their children.

These traditional mindsets have evolved into the gender roles we still see today. The industrial revolution along with the digital age has lessened the necessity of these roles. As we conquer our environment the need for strong family systems has devolved into an option rather than a requirement for survival. Role reversals have increased in frequency with more women financially supporting the family while the male stays home to raise the children, or the total absence of a male whatsoever. Masculinity is viewed as toxic in some circles, while femininity has been redefined as a dominant trait.

These blurred lines have intensified over the last few generations leaving today's children with no clear guide as to what is naturally expected of their birth sex. Where gender once aligned with sex, many now view it as an option that can be changed on a whim. Unless you are born with no traces of reproductive organs or significant properties of both, you cannot change your birth sex. Behavior, clothing, facial hair, breasts, all traits associated with binary sex can be altered chemically or with surgery. None of these alterations change your sex, only how you present yourself to the world. This presentation has been described as gender identity. A less often used but more appropriate term is disguise.

People often disguise themselves as something they are not. Some put all their resources into expensive clothes and cars while living on a friend's couch. I once worked with a mechanic that would scrub his hands after work until they bled. His fear was that the wealthy people he associated with would learn that he worked with his hands. This was no small fear; he was fanatically terrified of his financial position being revealed. I once joked that all gay guys are wealthy, and that I wasn't sure how many same sex encounters he would have to enact to obtain wealth, but it would make him rich. He paused for a long moment as he processed the possibility. Had my solution been plausible he would have jumped on it. The point is that people will go to extremes to present themselves as they wish to be seen as an identity. Social media has amplified this need for an appealing persona to attract as much attention from a targeted group as possible.

The need to belong is a powerful force, it can make people turn their back on family and friends. Gender identity, religion, cults, conspiracy theory, politics, the list goes on forever. People can easily lose their true self in the pursuit of an alternate identity or belief they find appealing. Repetitious exposure to an ideology attracts the Id, which pushes the Ego to rationalize it to the Superego.

An effective message repeated often enough can eventually override our sense of self resulting in a hive mentality. In this world a person surrounds themselves with others repeating mantras and statements that reinforce their ideology. Competitive spirit often induces members of the group to vie for the post of sincerest believer, performing sacrifices of comfort or marking their body to proclaim their sincerity. A gang tattoo or bumper sticker are milder examples of sincerity; chemical or surgical procedures are the more extreme. Most of America was shocked to find a cult that had castrated themselves before committing suicide so their spirits could travel on a spaceship. Now we have medical associations that celebrate children and their parents demanding chemical alterations and surgical amputations.

A lesser percentage of this group have nominal mental capacity, but many of them have less than the normal ability to function, often proclaiming they are on the spectrum. What chance do mentally challenged children and their misguided parents have against advanced algorithms and gang mentality? In the next chapter we'll cover the less fortunate of us.

The Spectrum

As a population, approximately 68 percent of people are considered within normal cognitive function and intelligence. Using a zero-centerline reference on a graph, anyone 34 percent below or above this line is considered within normal range. Anyone above this 34 percent of the centerline is considered advanced, gifted or genius. Anyone below the lesser 34 percent is traditionally referred to as challenged or delayed. The word "retarded", once used descriptively for the mentally impaired in levels of mild, moderate and severe, has been removed from diagnostic terminology. This was due to the derogatory use of the expression as a slur used with cruel intent.

The current preferred expression is "on the spectrum", borrowed from autism spectrum disorder. The word spectrum was most used to separate various types of light sorted by their wave lengths on a linier scale. The word also defines degrees between two points of reference. In its current medical application these two points refer to less than the negative 34 percentile and bottom out at no signs of intelligence or conscious thought.

Neurotypical describes the average person's ability to perceive, process and apply information to perform tasks or to communicate within what are considered normal parameters. This includes typical speech patterns, movement of the body, extremities and facial expressions. Neurodiversity is a non-medical term that describes people with non-typical brain function. The neurodiverse brain perceives, processes and responds differently from the norm. These differences can be very subtle or in some cases extreme. The National Cancer Institute estimates that 15 to 20 percent of the world population has some form of neurodivergence. In its milder form, being neurodivergent can be advantageous. Having a brain that is wired different can result in advanced thought processes. They are finely tuned to interpret and apply math, produce music, art, or master many languages. Neurodivergence in its extreme negative form can result in behavior that is self-harming, non-verbal or nonfunctioning altogether.

Causes of neurodivergence range from physical trauma to the brain during or post birth, brain chemistry, genetics, genetic disorder or birth defect. Other contributing factors to this condition are older birth parents, preterm birth, low birth weight, frequent infections, prenatal exposure to toxins such as tobacco, alcohol, and pollutants. Regardless of the cause, approximately one in five people have this condition to some degree.

Since many highly functioning neurodivergent people have an average or higher intelligence, IQ is not a direct determining factor in diagnosis. Autism spectrum disorder can present itself in any number of symptoms and degrees. Avoiding eye contact, inability to start or maintain a conversation, vocal ticks, erratic and/or repetitive movements, clumsiness, strong reaction to loud sounds or bright light, and learning disabilities to name a few. Fixation or obsession with a single subject or object is also a common symptom.

Recent advancements in testing have identified many neurological disorders and is often cited as the main contributing factor to the current high percentage of neurodivergent detected in our population. This does not take into consideration that medical advances have altered the human condition once dominated solely by nature. In 1880 the child mortality rate was 347 out of 1000 live births. Over a third of children born did not reach the age of five. By 1920 child mortality was halved to 185 per 1000. Since the invention of penicillin in 1928 and other medical advances there has been a steep decline in child mortality. By 2020 the mortality rate of live births stabilized to 7 in 1000. In the mid 1960's children born a month or more prematurely stood a much lower chance of surviving infancy than today.

The CDC states current premature births average around 10%. When we say premature that means birth before the medically calculated due date. Most assume this means 9 months after fertilization, but it is closer to ten. By the time women confirm they are pregnant a month has passed leaving nine months to complete a full-term birth. In full term birth (40 weeks) the liver, lungs and brain have had every chance to fully develop. The final weeks and days are critical to this development. Any birth before 37 weeks is considered preterm. Child births of 32 weeks or less have a higher probability of cerebral palsy, breathing, hearing, vision and neurological problems. Babies with low birth weight may exhibit the same results. Preterm birth and low birth weight are associated with 14 percent of infant deaths before the age of one.

Many Neurodiverse have other health issues besides neural. A substantial number have problematic births that would have resulted in low survivability two hundred years ago. In nature these people would never have the opportunity to reproduce and pass on their faulty genetics to their children and grandchildren. This was nature's way of weeding out the weaker genes from being passed on.

Parental age is also a prominent factor that has been linked to autism. Our cells constantly replicate, after so many replications some cells are not perfect duplicates called free radicals. After the age of 30 male sperm is more likely to carry more mutations caused by these free radicals. According to Raheleh Rahbari at the Wellcome Sanger Institute in the UK Oct 2025, A male in his early 30's sperm count has a 1 in 50 ratio of disease causing mutations. These are referred to as selfish sperm. Selfish means that they are more likely to pierce the ovum shell and successfully conceive, winning the race against healthy sperm without anomalies. They found 40 genes that when mutated cause this selfish reaction, many have no significant result but two are directly linked to autism. By age 70 these selfish sperm are more common at a 1 in 20 ratio. These findings were significant enough that the doctors recommend men that plan to have children after the age of thirty should freeze their sperm at an earlier age to avoid the likelihood of neural and physical anomalies in their offspring.

A large portion of people walking the earth today owe their existence to modern science. In nature, without these advances nearly 40% of us would never have seen our fifth birthday. Darwin and Spencer's theory "survival of the fittest" has been redirected to any chance of survivability. A large portion of the neurodivergent born today would never have survived birth or lived past their fifth birthday two hundred years ago.

These biologically/mentally atypical people (with inheritable genetic mutations) have reproduced exponentially. Between environmental factors, birth trauma, older parents, and in large part genetics, neurodivergence is more prolific now than any other time in our history. It's simply how we are now as a population. The downfall of this is that a significant number of people do not process information normally and tend to fixate or obsess in a detrimental manner. They are vulnerable to algorithms and irregular ideas that are constantly repeated within their sphere of information.

Most people on the spectrum know they are different. They've spent their life struggling through a faulty brain to understand, communicate, feel and experience what everyone else takes for granted. Just to formulate an appropriate sentence can take a massive effort, leaving little time for the next words after a response from others. After a while many just withdraw into themselves with frustration and settle for being a social outcast.

Suddenly a bright light illuminates the world, and a life raft appears to save these poor souls drowning in sorrow and loneliness. And its name is social media. They can take the time to prepare a script and make a video saying what they want, comment on what others say, and have that social interaction all humans crave. If you can type and post pictures, you'll soon be embraced by a circle of friends like yourself. Discussing topics and ideas the normies would never bother with. Some social awkwardness is acceptable but there are boundaries that shouldn't be challenged lest the wrath of your online friends be wrought upon you. One of those boundaries is challenging the group's opinion on identity. For most people in the physically interactive world, identity is their name and personality. In the world of social media, it's your moniker and online reputation.

Online identity is very important to someone dependent on social media as their sole means of interacting with others. When someone introduces the concept of gender identity, some will be puzzled but go along with the group to avoid making waves in their happy space. Others will get excited and supply links to trans influencers that prance and wiggle in front of their cameras proclaiming how happy they are.

Many influencers make a good living off their sales pitch. They proclaim how unhappy and alone they were before finding their true selves through brave acts of sacrifice. Just click like or follow to begin your journey towards true bliss. Come join a community of millions just like you where you can celebrate being your true self.

Soon some in the group start identifying as trans and others follow not wanting to be left out of the loop. More links appear and the discussions begin to center around particular statements made by the influencers. You must click the link to see what everyone in your circle is talking about. You must learn the terms and phrases everyone is using. That's when those devious algorithms take over and your whole social life soon consists of repetitive messages promising the cure to all of life's problems.

In the old days this was called brain washing and it is effective. Subliminal messages were at one time placed in film for one or two frames throughout the movie, subconsciously coercing you to buy from the snack bar. If a normal mind can be pushed towards an alternate reality through repetitive suggestion, what chance do the neurodivergent have? Next, we will address the people that should know better.

The Medical Community

Medical Boards were created to ensure properly trained and licensed health care providers could tend to patients' needs. They have set a very strict minimum high standard of care in the U.S. Each state has its' own medical boards, which anyone practicing medicine must be registered to practice in. Individual states may have stricter regulations or require additional qualifications.

There are a multitude of these medical boards governing nurses, pharmacists, specialists, and mental health to name a few. We've been taught since childhood to respect and trust educated people of authority. We trust our doctors with our health and often with our lives. This includes our mental health. A medical doctor can specialize in psychiatry and can become a psychiatrist. They have the advantage of thoroughly understanding and treating the human body and the mind. A psychologist has the same fundamental understanding of the mind without the full medical background of an MD. A counselor has far less training than either and provides services more akin to life coaching. They can counsel one on one, married couples, hold group sessions, counsel addicts and a list of social services. All three do require licensing and yearly minimum studies to maintain their license.

Medical boards not only ensure quality of health care for patients, they also regulate and monitor the behavior of medical providers. If a new procedure, treatment or medication may be financially and physically beneficial to providers and patients the individual boards will scrutinize all available information before they approve it. Their approval goes a long way in procuring payment from the insurance companies. In many cases an FDA approved medication may be useful in treating maladies it was not originally designed for. This is known as off label use. Drug manufacturers make huge investments to properly develop and test their products only to be shot down by the FDA if their product is too unsafe or inefficient in its intended purpose.

In double blind studies the participants and the researchers do not know who are getting the medicine or the placebo. In this way the participants do not alter their behavior affecting the outcome. As opposed to single blind where the researcher knows which is the placebo and may unintentionally signal which group the participant is in causing biased outcomes.

What a boon to a drug manufacturer to discover that a medication approved for one malady may also be beneficial for others. Their return on investment grows exponentially as doctors successfully prescribe their drug for other off label ailments or conditions. One such current popular drug is used for treating diabetes. It slows digestion resulting in weight loss that will improve anyone's health simply through the loss of weight. It also curbs addictions to some degree. These health benefits must be weighed against the possible side effects, such as intestinal paralysis and pancreatitis.

This will be a long-term treatment since most patients taken off this medication will put the weight back on. Why so, because you're mostly treating symptoms and not the cause of obesity, usually poor eating habits and lack of exercise. For some people's body chemistry, it is the only solution, for others it is easier than practicing self-control. Still others that have discontinued this drug's use may continue their healthier habits because they now see the benefits. Either way it will improve most people's health if it is not abused as in the case of prescribing it to a thin person with anorexia. In this situation it is not in the patient's best interest to encourage or affirm unhealthy behavior.

Medical boards may or may not approve procedures or therapies with the same scrutiny the FDA applies to drugs. Groups of doctors in the medical or psychological fields may band together to promote certain ideals they personally believe in, then lobby for the medical board's approval. Once a procedure or therapy is accepted by the boards the insurance companies will usually support financial responsibility. Special interest groups may recruit large numbers of doctors to lobby on their behalf to encourage odd procedures or off-label use of certain medications. There may be valid research to justify uncommon or expensive treatments that have yet to be approved.

The more doctors and researchers that promote these techniques the better chance they will have for a board's recommendation or the medical community's acceptance. Some doctors may lobby on behalf of their own best interests, publishing incomplete or biased data to attract patients to their practice. They may honestly believe they are helping alleviate suffering while promoting elective therapies and procedures as essential treatments. Whether these doctors truly believe in the needs of their patients or are simply opportunists, they are knowingly exposing healthy people to unnecessary bodily harm. Harm that can result in irreversible lifelong consequences. Some states medical boards may elect to ban certain procedures or medications they deem ineffective or unsafe.

Now let's talk about one special interest group that has altered the medical, social and political landscape in recent years. The World professional Association for Transgender Health or WPATH. The title sounds rather authoritarian, emanating respect as a worldwide association of professionals. There are many professional members, and for 200.00 a year anyone else can be a professional member too. This organization started out as the Harry Benjamin International Gender Dysphoria Association in 1979. A collection of like-minded therapists and psychologists that contributed to the initial version of the Standards Of Care (SOC).

Harry Benjamin first published his theories in 1966 recognizing transsexualism as a mental condition and labeling it incurable. The basis for his publication centers on the theory that true transsexualism is innate and not in need of any cure. His earlier medical background included performing a partial vasectomy which he claimed restored youthful energy and libido. Studying sexual pathologies, he concluded that Transvestites (people that dressed as the opposite sex for sexual gratification), differed from transexuals that wished to become the opposite sex (gender identity disorder).

Benjamin concluded that psychoanalysis had no effect on the innate desire transexuals have to become the opposite sex. Though the common consensus at the time had established a 70% psychoanalytical success rate. His research led him to believe this 70% were not true transexuals. He suggested many patients also pretended to respond to reparative therapy while hiding their true desires causing severe distress (dysphoria). He sponsored the idea that it was better to change the body to match the desire, rather than treat the mind to accept biological reality. His first edition standards of care required intensive evaluation to establish a patient's condition before committing to any affirming therapy which includes cross dressing, hormone and/or surgical treatments.

This enraged many in the transexual community as a form of regulation from the medical establishment. The initial reception of the standards of care in the medical field was a mix of criticism and revelation. These were new ideas that ran contrary to established psychological protocol. Yet if you accept that it is an incurable condition, shouldn't you make an incurable patient as comfortable as possible? Let's just feed into this denial of physical reality and affirm (confirm) that transsexuals are justified in rejecting the body they were born with. Let's then chemically and surgically alter their body to comfort their delusion. Are these doctors treating the symptoms or the illness?

This is all well and good if you accept the key word in this theory (innate). Innate means born that way, not learned behavior. Everyone is born with a blank slate. No one is born with a predetermined belief or behavior incongruent to their physical make up. Most behavior is learned either by example, observation, attraction or imagination. Instinctual behavior is a survival mechanism that is mostly constructive and usually advantageous. Men instinctually protect the women and offspring; women nurture the children and protect the family unit. What instinctive advantage is obtained with the dissociation of your body? If transsexualism is not instinctive, then it must be learned behavior. Some genetic disorders affect testosterone production or absorption. This can lead to less aggressive behavior or less masculine features. It does not negate instinct or birth sex.

Before social media made transsexualism fashionable, it was an exceedingly rare aberration. Many transexuals claim dissatisfactions with their condition to the point of suicidal idealizations. Most caring people would take this as a cry for help in need of a reparative remedy, not a wonderful opportunity to be exploited. This is where the human element becomes evident.

Everyone sees the world through their own eyes. This means I am the center of the world and everyone else is compared to my standard. If I am gay or bi, then everybody else must be, they just don't act on it, or society has stifled their ability to be their true selves. If I am trans, then I am one of the lucky few in touch with my true self. This would mean everyone in disagreement is either closed-minded, unenlightened, or too cowardly to admit their personal truth. This mindset tasks the individual to incorporate others into their beliefs. The more people of like minds you can gather, the more self-justified your beliefs become.

Once you've convinced a large number of people to share your view, your belief becomes a cause or movement. The movement evolves into a belief based following of like minds. Secure in the power of numbers, this movement now demands respect and recognition, making demands on converts as well as outsiders. Key words and phrases become your orientation and your mantra. You're either with us or against us. We demand everyone respects our importance and self-imposed titles (pronouns) and beliefs.

We must be free to spread the word in schools and libraries so we can recruit others to join us and our cause. How can children ever learn about this new freedom unless it's taught at the earliest age possible? Society is so very wrong with its archaic beliefs that are contrary to this brave next phase of human social evolution. There is no room for God in this new world. And for those that persist in spirituality, "God made me Trans, and I am perfect" is the new acceptable tagline. Pick your side, enemy or ally, ignorant hater or enlightened revolutionary. The greatest folly of human nature comes to a head; it's us or them. Welcome to the family or woe be onto you if you attract our ire.

As more of these more radicalized zealots became physicians, lawyers and researchers, they swelled the roster at WPATH while contributing their gender supportive research, philosophies and beliefs. Subtle changes to the Standards of Care evolved into a fringe manifesto. The tone of the organization shifted from medically oriented to a radicalized sect with credentials. The new trans leadership which had taken over WPATH by 2007 wielded their political and medical influence as a cudgel. The inmates were now running the asylum. This well-organized movement continued expanding on multiple fronts. To extend their membership, they recruited the LGB faction of society.

The LGB is based on sexual attraction, while the trans community embraces refusal to accept their birth sex. Although there were always a few LGB that wished to experience being the opposite sex, attraction to someone born with the same equipment is the standard requirement to be a core LGB member. The Trans movement slipped in using sympathy. Reminding the LGB that being same sex attraction was once considered a mental illness, now the same considerations should be applied to trans. This merger of beliefs was mostly advantageous to the trans community and not so much for the LGB. Originally adding a "T" for trans to the initials (LGBT) they later added other initials from the odd and disenfranchised that evolved into the current alphabet LGBTQIA+.

This takeover demanded complete fealty to the movement, including various new flags, rules and terminology. Mob mentality now ruled the progressive movement, ready to violently turn on anyone with less than a fanatical allegiance to the cause. Don't support trans women in sports, puberty blockers, cross hormone treatments, or decide to detransition and expect to be ostracized, attacked online, in person, or have SWAT sent to your home. Meanwhile, WPATH affiliated lawyers showed up in the courts to argue against any perceived slight that may question their beliefs or intent. This community then spread to the furthest corners of the world with similar effects.

Here in America, WPATH members were occupying medical and psychological boards beginning in 2010. Gaining respect in both communities they offered a new flow of income from the insurance companies. Garnering approval for affirming therapy such as medicinal and surgical procedures including amputations, body and facial reconstruction, vocal therapy and hair removal. All these procedures previously considered elective were now frequently covered by Medicaid and some private insurance. Trans patients were covered for procedures that the general public were not. Puberty blockers and hormone treatments for juveniles were distributed by newly opened gender clinics spreading across the country. Staffed by believers in the cause, these treatments set children up for a lifetime of medications their body did not require. Side effects were played down or ignored since the only other result would be suicide if not immediately prescribed. Or so they claimed.

Not every doctor or therapist in the gender field callously pushed patients into transitioning, although many trans have stated they received hormones after one office visit. Others seeking transition with responsible gender specialists complained about how long it took to be properly evaluated. Different doctors have different approaches when following SOC guidelines. Some may bypass thorough evaluation recommendations or simply sign off on a PA's or RN recommendation.

In some cases, if a child expressed concern that they had feelings for the same sex and questioned if they were gay, the gender counselor could offer an alternative solution. Telling them they were not gay, just a straight person trapped in the wrong body, "Now let's get you started on hormones right away before you hurt yourself." Of course, you'll need a new name and different clothes. With multiple sessions we can save your life! Parents were conscripted to advocate for and practice these beliefs in affirmation. Extended family, neighbors, schools and local government had to be notified and coerced by any means necessary to ensure this new identity was respected and reinforced to avoid any discomfort to the patient.

Some counselors boasted online of recommending a symbolic funeral for their patients' previous self while being born anew as the opposite sex with a new name and pronouns. This social revolution brought out the worse fanatics trying to make a name for themselves with ridiculous claims. One urologist claimed that all urinals should be removed because men empty their bladders better sitting down as opposed to standing. An anthropologist claimed identifying male and female skeletons by sex was impossible since they were identical. Children should be encouraged to imagine themselves as minotaurs, furries, gender fluid or non-binary. Social norms were labeled archaic and damaging to all children with their unnatural expectations.

WPATH members went to court in multiple states successfully outlawing reparative therapy, relabeling it conversion therapy. WPATH claim these corrective therapies are wrong and damaging to the patient. Somehow, overlooking that they were pushing their own cult like conversion therapy. One based on fantasy and faulty theory rather than reality and fact. In some states child custody and adoptions were decided solely on acceptance of gender theory established by WPATH guidelines.

The liberal leaning government at the time needed all the votes they could get. A trans was elected to congress, another was put in charge of HHS and immediately insisted on using any bathroom they wanted, sanctioning anyone not using correct self-imposed pronouns. Women and girls' sports and locker rooms were invaded by males claiming to be female, proudly exposing themselves and justifying it with two magic words, "I'm trans". Any attempt to separate males from females in sports or private areas was met with faulty data claiming no physical advantage or differences. The gender movement claimed trans women not winning every time in competition stood as analytical proof that they held no physical advantage over natural women.

The terms natural or normal men and women made the trans community uncomfortable, so they demanded a different term "cis gender" be used instead. Twenty new pronouns, unlimited possible genders plus non-binary and gender fluid, this movement wanted to label everyone while claiming persecution if you label them. In some countries the terms mother and father need to be avoided because they are considered insensitive and cause distress to the LGBTQIA+ community. The word vagina was renamed the third hole by those that could not have a real vagina or disliked being born with one.

Liberal news channels and social media endorsed WPATHs' beliefs as the law of the land accepted by every doctor in the medical community. Any publicly dissenting medical professional was publicly exposed and discredited with their license to practice called into question. One such doctor performed a study of rapid onset gender dysphoria. This study confirmed a direct relationship between social media and the sudden increase in numbers of gender dysphoria in children ages 10 and up. Originally published in Scientific American, a host of WPATH professionals immediately scrutinized the results demanding the paper be retracted. Not because of scientific process, but because one peer signature was missing and a flaw was found in the patient informed consent form. Under pressure the publication publicly retracted the findings and the gender theory community celebrated by claiming the study had been fully debunked. Doctors involved in the study were ostracized and their professional careers stained to teach others not to make waves.

If WPATH were truly a medically professional driven organization, wouldn't they study these results and admit the possibility? It could serve as a useful tool in avoiding misdiagnosis. No, because they control the narrative, only they get to say what makes people trans. They claim you must be trans to understand that it is innate, that trans are born that way and incurable. In fact, they don't need a cure, they are perfectly normal. Say differently and watch what happens to you.

Many colleges medical courses were now required to include trans sensitivity training. This was for the comfort of patients that require a delicate series of questions to properly identify their birth sex. Men and women have different medical needs and proper identification of birth sex is critical to their optimum care. As an example, a husky bearded man came into an emergency room complaining about abdominal pain. By the time they found out the patient was a pregnant biological woman the baby was lost. Now who is at fault in this situation, the patient encouraged (affirmed) to believe they were a man? Can a man have a functional vagina and perform coitus as a woman, then be ignorant of the physiological possibility that pregnancy could occur? Yet still present themselves as a man while a human life was lost. It becomes obvious that feeding delusion is not always in an individual's best interest or the interest of others.

This is where reality should be prioritized over identity. Sure, go ahead and identify as the opposite sex, but know you have certain physical attributes that cannot be ignored. Hormones and surgeries can complicate this even further when physicians need to know what patient sex and alterations they're dealing with for an accurate prognosis.

There are many well intentioned doctors that try to do what is best for trans patients that also belong to WPATH. In 2024 the WPATH files were released revealing conversations between responsible doctors questioning the S.O.C. guidelines and ethics. Their concerns included children requesting transition with no concept of biology, or the magnitude of physical stress and permanent damage their body would suffer. In most cases the parents were just as naive.

Other concerns included children with autism and other more severe psychological issues that should be addressed before assessing a child for transition. In most instances the response was to ignore obvious psychological disorders and immediately address the child's request with the guidelines set out in the S.O.C. which includes immediate affirmation therapy. The well-meaning doctors were spoken down to as if lacking compassion. A video of this can be found online. Simply search "the WPATH files" and see it for yourself. WPATH is not the science based irrefutable fact-based organization they claim to be. It now operates as a social, political and cultural philosophy disguised as science. When other countries took it upon themselves to do their own research, they found many discrepancies in WPATHs evidence-based claims. The Cass report compiled in England being the most thorough to date.

Dr Hillary Cass conducted a thorough scientific evaluation of the issues transgender citizens were experiencing in England's health care system. This was a study initiated with an aggressive approach to evaluate the best treatment for transgender people in the U.K. Part of that study involved all current available studies and publications including those present in the SOC published by WPATH. Also drawing from her own pool of interviews with trans patients, care givers, pharmaceutical test results, and England's health care data base. In conclusion Dr Cass found that cross sex hormones and puberty blockers are not safe or substantially monitored over time as many trans advocates claim. Nor are the risks of these side effects negated by the range of benefits claimed by prescribing these medications to children.

Surgical intervention which is never 100% reversable should never be applied to anyone under the age of 18. Over 90% of the claimed evidence-based studies listed by WPATH did not pass scientific muster. This includes WPATH's core theory, that people are just born that way. And to prove that is a false statement in WPATH's own words, *"The expression of gender characteristics, including identities, that are not stereotypically associated with one's sex assigned at birth is a common and a culturally diverse human phenomenon that should not be seen as inherently negative or pathological"*. This is a direct quote from page 8 of the S.O.C. version 8. It is the first paragraph under the subtitle Diversity versus Diagnosis. The key word here is phenomenon, which means, a fact or situation that is observed to exist or happen, especially one whose cause or explanation is in question. A common synonym of phenomenon is a miracle.

Everything WPATH is based on, the core principle of trans theory and treatment hinges on an unexplained observation or phenomenon. They cannot explain or prove their observations origins and cannot prove it is an innate condition. This brings up the question, is transsexualism incurable? Is affirmation therapy the only appropriate treatment? This unconfirmed concept started from theory one man promoted in a book over sixty years ago. And rather than question or test that theory which any scientific mind would normally do, a large group of professionals (WPATH) stomp their feet and proclaim," Because we say so"! That is not sound logic, it is an opinion based on bias and willful ignorance.

The Cass report was viciously attacked by multiple WPATH professionals and trans activists, claiming the report was biased because there were no trans team leaders included in the analytical process. Other accusations listed in "An Evidence-Based Critique of the Cass Review" from Yale, claimed the report misinterprets and misrepresents its own data, has serious methodological flaws, and my favorite, "page 4 *Section 1: The Cass Review makes statements that are consistent with the models of gender-affirming medical care described by WPATH and the Endocrine Society. The Cass Review does not recommend a ban on gender-affirming medical care."*

That's right, they criticized Dr. Cass's methodology and competency, then twisted the report's findings and recommendations into an endorsement of WPATHs methods because Dr Cass did not specifically recommend a ban. It should be mentioned here that Yale issued a statement that their school of medicine does not endorse this critique. Somehow that part was conveniently left out.

Affirming Therapy and Results

WPATH updates the SOC every so often to conform to the social landscape and whatever may be perceived as a need in the LGBTQIA+ community. Their current guidelines are labeled version 8. Any reference to SOC recommendations will be accompanied by page number in the version 8 SOC available on the WPATH.org website. That way any individual can confirm nothing has been taken out of context.

Let's start with the medications. Traditional medications are applied to either treat or prevent an illness, injury or condition that will adversely affect or cause pain, discomfort or harm to an individual. Since the beginning of time certain plants and minerals were discovered that could treat common human ailments. Alcohol, stimulants and opiates are among the oldest, while other elements were more specific in their application.

Nature provides many natural cures in roots, plants, berries, and seeds. Our early ancestors discovered what medicines worked best and handed this information down for generations. Many of these remedies were toxic without proper refinement or deadly if too much were applied. The process of removing the active ingredient may have amplified the desired results but sometimes tended to remove other elements that made the cure more tolerant for the body. Dosage and frequency of application are critical to effectiveness and safety of the patient along with individual tolerance to avoid allergic reactions. Age and weight of the patient must also be factored in. The ancient alchemists made a pretty penny developing these cures and treatments.

Now let's discuss hormones. These are molecules naturally produced in the human body by glands that control or regulate different bodily functions. There are over 60 hormones constantly controlling bodily functions along with 12 steroids. Steroids differ in make-up and are cholesterol based. All steroids are hormones, but not all hormones are steroids because of these differences. All hormones act as chemical messengers spread through the body by blood flow or interconnecting systems. On a cellular level they control weight, fluid retention, growth, sugar level, and behavior to mention a few functions.

Adrenaline is a prime example of a fast-acting hormone that everyone has experienced. With the same speed adrenaline is dispersed, most hormones are rapidly adjusted by glands using a feedback system to regulate the proper levels according to the body's needs. Too much or too little sugar in the blood and the pancreas will release different amounts of insulin to help the body maintain a healthy balance.

An imbalance of any hormone can have life altering effects. Some medications assist glands in performing better, directly treating the cause of an imbalance at its source. When such treatment is not an option, hormone replacement therapy is the next alternative. Diabetes type 2 can often be treated with medications, but if correct levels cannot be obtained insulin injections may be required along with consistent level monitoring.

From the early stages of life many different combinations of hormones flood the body to promote muscle development, bone density, sexual maturity, and brain growth while strictly controlling the cellular response throughout the body. Hormone levels such as testosterone and estrogen escalate during puberty, once the body has matured, these higher levels are no longer needed, and most glands settle into a maintenance mode monitoring and correcting hormone levels throughout our body's lifetime. Different conditions can affect this delicate system that controls every cell in our body. Poor nutrition, inactivity, or injury can overwhelm one or more gland's ability to correct chemical imbalances. Alcohol consumption, smoking, pollutants and genetics also contribute to glandular irregularities along with age. At any time after birth any gland can fail to operate correctly or cease function altogether often with catastrophic results.

One hormone classified as a steroid is testosterone. Both sexes have the presence of testosterone and estrogen in their body. All female eggs carry the X chromosome, while sperm can carry either a Y or X chromosome. If the fertilizing sperm shares a Y chromosome the baby will be a male with XY paired chromosomes. If the fertilizing sperm carries an X the result will be XX pairing which indicates a female. Embryos are identical in appearance for the first six weeks until the Y chromosome induces the creation of high testosterone levels. This begins the formation of male genitalia from an area known as the genital ridge. Genetically female embryos develop female genitalia from the same ridge driven by the presence of estrogen. In male embryos testosterone can reach levels of a grown man until 16-24 weeks after conception when levels drop until early puberty. If not for testosterone induced by the Y chromosome all babies would be born female, and humanity would cease to exist. About one in a thousand embryos develop intersex traits during this phase that will be noticeable at birth. Research suggests that almost two percent of the population have subtle genetic and/or hormonal conditions that vary from the typical binary system of sexual classification. These subtle atypical conditions tend to show up at puberty or sometimes later in life. One rare condition occurs when one embryo absorbs another causing two sets of XX and XY chromosomes. Regardless of some anomalies, the Y chromosome, and the resulting testosterone levels are the deciding factor in male sexual development.

Puberty begins at age 11 on average but can start as early as age 9 or as late as 14. During this time testosterone levels climb, and the male begins to mature in stages. Testosterone is a growth hormone causing the addition of muscle mass, bone and genital growth, pubic hair and an increase in strength along with deepening of voice. Mood swings are also evident since hormones directly affect behavior. These physiological changes attributed to puberty will continue until they level off by the age of sixteen or seventeen.

Skeletal maturity will be reached at this time in males, while female skeletal maturity will be reached earlier 13-15 years. From birth, our bones are not as solid as most would imagine. Long bone structure (arms and legs) until the early 20's are mostly soft cartilage and spongy bone towards the outer ends known as growth plates. This is where bone growth takes place as the bone lengthens. Once skeletal maturity is reached these plates ossify (calcify and harden) creating a solid outer bone with cartilage remaining as the cushion between joints. Spinal growth is similar as each vertebrae has its own growth plate elongating in size as well as lateral growth until maturity. This stage of puberty is critical in forming a healthy skeleton and joint formation.

Precocious puberty is a condition where children start puberty before the typical age. Children with this condition will display all the signs of puberty before the body is normally ready for it. Rapid growth and early sexual development not only start early but also tend to end early. Compared to normal development where a gradual height is reached before the pubertal growth spurt. Precocious children reach full height earlier with a lower starting point. In the long run they tend to be shorter in stature than their peers. Bone formation and density may also be affected by this early development. Causes of precocious puberty range from genetics, tumors, brain injuries, obesity, and sometimes simply can't be isolated. It is much more common in females and non-Caucasian populations. Treatments usually involve puberty blockers to allow the body's prepubescent growth to complete before puberty begins.

Testosterone and estrogen are the main hormones involved in puberty and growth while serving other reproductive purposes later in life. A part of the brain called the hypothalamus releases the gonadotropin-releasing hormone (GnRH) which triggers the pituitary gland to release luteinizing hormone (LH). LH then travels to testes in males stimulating testosterone production, and the ovaries in females stimulating the production of estrogen and progesterone. This is a very precise process which was discovered in early research. Once GnRH was identified and synthesized in the lab its medicinal value was assessed for practical applications. Synthetic testosterone and estrogen have some unwanted side effects. The opportunity to enhance the bodies triggering mechanisms to create natural testosterone and estrogen would be a much safer alternative.

When GnRH was administered to the test subjects of both sexes, testosterone and estrogen release stopped. Further research confirmed as with similar products, that gonad stimulation only occurred when GnRH was released in precise pulses or spurts separated by precisely timed intervals. Outside of a mechanical device accurately injecting GnRH 24 hours a day, the medicinal applications were now limited. If the required result was to eliminate production of these hormones, then synthetic GnRH had a medicinal value.

Treating precocious puberty was an ideal application. It was much faster acting than similar LH blockers which included the birth control and chemical castration drug MPA, that was developed in the 1950's. GnRH is a preferred treatment for prostate cancer compared with estrogen therapy and surgical castration. When GnRH is used as prescribed for precocious (early) puberty, the body is given the chance to fully develop to the stage where puberty should begin. The drug is then discontinued, and the patient develops at a rate relative to their peers.

Puberty is a hormone driven physical stage the body experiences as it begins to mature. Growth spurts, change in genitalia, pubic hair, along with the development of breasts and menstruation for girls, voice deepening and emissions for the boys are observed during puberty. Add the flood of hormones saturating the brain and it can be a very stressful experience for the average child. To the less stable young mind it can become a stage of life fraught with consternation.

For a child with gender identity disorder, puberty represents the end of disillusionment. Now faced with the reality that they will fully develop into the sex they were born to become, abject fear can set in. Traditional therapy would reassure the patient that all this confusion is normal and natural, just let it happen and everything will be fine. Every adult has been through puberty and benefited from it in the long run, but the SOC says differently. Rebranding GnRH as puberty blockers, SOC 8 guidelines recommend prescribing GnRH meds to qualified trans children at the first signs of puberty. Claiming this gives them time to explore their gender identity and is totally reversable page s112 statement 12.1. This will also therapeutically alleviate stress levels from body changes.

Puberty serves multiple purposes. Every day of puberty the bones grow and ossify, the brain develops towards maturity, and the stress children go through are a part of their emotional growth. To pause this process months or a year robs the child of critical physical, mental and emotional development. The body does extend puberty duration in response to this chemically induced pause. To claim it's totally reversable is blatantly false. A loss is a loss, not a delay. A two year pause in puberty are two years of emotional development deprived of the elevated hormone levels in natural emotional growth. Blockers are commonly used until the mid-teens when cross hormone treatment begins to further circumvent natural growth. The advocates for chemical affirmation therapy say the end justify the risks, including the follow up of hormone therapy that have documented side effects. Let us not overlook that no long-term scientific studies have been made of non-precocious children exposed to puberty blockers into their later years.

When Dr. Cass made these observations, she was harshly criticized by WPATH. You would think medical professionals would take her findings into account and conduct further research. Fearing the results of further research, WPATH supporters would rather just criticize Cass's findings.

Many children requesting these medical interventions have no concept of basic biology, they only know what they heard online, from friends or a gender advocate. How can they make an informed decision that will affect them the rest of their lives? After girls start cross sex hormone therapy their voice deepens and they develop facial hair, the vaginal wall thins and can atrophy.

Boys' taking estrogen experience low sperm count, testicular atrophy (long term treatment) and genitals that don't fully develop. Male orgasm may never be experienced in these patients along with low libido. There have been reports of males on estrogen feeling pain like broken glass when erect. Had these natural males been allowed to flourish through normal puberty their choices about transition may well be different. Eliminating the ability to have an orgasm for a lifetime is no small matter. The thought of an erection feeling like broken glass isn't very appealing either. Do you really think every child is fully advised of these possible side effects?

WPATH's guidelines would add to the fear of approaching pubertal changes. They put a negative focus on the changes a child's body will go through unless puberty is stopped. They then offer an alternative that is not in young patients' best physical interests. A lifelong sentence of serum steroids the body does not normally require. This may be a personal choice for an adult, but not for a child with a child's mentality. Cass recommended not prescribing puberty blockers or cross hormone therapy to children under the age of 18 unless in a clinical study.

Dr. Cass also noted the high percentage of trans having other cognizant or emotional issues indicating gender incongruence as another symptom rather than the cause of gender distress. Transitioning is not a fix all cure for every juvenile discomfort. If WPATH were interested in their young patient's mental health, they would help them accept and love themselves for what and who they are, not what they wish to be. Encouraging anyone to be something they can never be is not only unethical but also cruel.

SOC version 8 includes a focus on children and adults that identify as eunuch. CHAPTER 9 pages88 Eunuchs *Among the many people who benefit from gender-affirming medical care, those who identify as eunuchs are among the least visible.* The 8th version of the Standards of Care (SOC) includes a discussion of eunuch individuals because of their unique presentation and their need for medically necessary gender-affirming care (see Chapter 2—Global Applicability, Statement 2.1)

This is an identity that applies to males only. This label does not include males that may have their testicles and or penis removed accidentally or from medical necessity.

Eunuch is recognized by WPATH as a legitimate gender identity that has been embraced by an individual which requires medically necessary gender-affirming care. According to SOC version 8, this is a perfectly ordinary frame of mind requiring medical intervention in the form of chemical or surgical castration to align a patients' body with their identity. Though many gender specialists refuse to treat this identity surgically, they have no problem performing the same techniques when transitioning a patient from male to trans female. The few doctors and clinics that will perform these eunuch surgical interventions label those refusing to perform eunuch surgeries hypocrites and impassionate. Maybe they refuse to indulge these patients because it is not within their ethical beliefs.

Eunuchs may identify as male, straight, gay, gender fluid, or non-binary. The ones identifying as male may not identify with the genitalia they were born with or find discomfort with the sexuality their sex organs imply. After castration many eunuchs express great relief knowing the offensive organs have been removed or neutralized. Whereas gender-fluid or non-binary patients may seek the total absence of genitalia (smoothies) or the surgical alternative of male and female genitalia (manufactured intersex). All these procedures are deemed medical necessities by WPATH to alleviate gender dysphoria. Dysphoria is a profound sense of unhappiness, distress, and indifference that can be a symptom of many mental health conditions. It is another word for anxiety.

In 1935 when confronted with a mental healthcare crisis a couple of doctors created a surgical procedure known as lobotomy. The originator of this first medically recognized lobotomy was later awarded the Nobel Prize in 1949. By drilling two holes in the skull and injecting alcohol to kill select brain cells, patients were relieved of their mental distress and dysphoria. Problems with how much brain matter was damaged resulted in an improved version known as the trans orbital lobotomy. The newer orbital version did not require the expense of a complete operating theater or surgical team. The only requirements to perform an orbital lobotomy were a sterile room, anesthesia or an electroshock machine to render the patient unconscious and an oversized icepick and a mallet.

The attending physician would push the icepick upward between the eyeball and eyelid. Using a hammer to tap through a thin layer of bone, the icepick is inserted into the brain and twisted while making a sweeping motion to separate the brain's frontal lobes from the rest of the brain. This procedure is repeated through the other eye cavity, completing the transorbital procedure. The operation lasted ten minutes and could be performed anywhere. Over 50,000 lobotomies were performed in the United States until 1967 when the medical boards banned the procedure based on poor long-term results and over 100 deaths. On rare occasions lobotomies may still be allowed in the most severe cases.

Severing parts of the brain seem very excessive to relieve dysphoria and other conditions now, but it was an acceptable and approved medical necessity for over 40 years. There is one notable difference between lobotomy and gender affirming therapies. Orbital lobotomy attempted to treat the cause of the distress at its source, the mind. Whereas gender affirming care justifies the minds fixation and alters the body to appease that fixation. Both methods were approved by the same medical community, and both cause physical harm to vulnerable patients.

Napoleon and Affirmation

Reality and perception can and do tend to coexist simultaneously. We use language to convey descriptions and information to each other. Every word has a definition which can change over time. Referring to an illness as a condition for instance. Medical definitions can change as new information is acquired, and a subject can be recategorized. Being LGB was listed as a mental disorder by the APA until 1973. Transsexualism (termed transgender) was delisted from the DSM (Diagnostic and Statistical Manual of Mental Disorders) in December of 2012. GID or gender identity disorder is now called gender incongruence. But they kept the term gender dysphoria meaning stress caused by gender incongruence as a diagnosis requiring treatment.

Gender theory supporters had been placed in the medical and psychology boards two years earlier initially as advisors. Now instead of an identity disorder trans are simply in disagreement with physical reality. This new terminology opened the door to our current situation with runaway hypochondriasis, where children amass online and self-diagnose as trans to form an identity. That does not mean there are not real transsexuals in the world, but it does diminish their credibility.

With this new radical social movement guiding and hiding in the WPATH organization with statements like SOC 8 page s 73 statement 7.8 *"The goal of psychotherapy should never be aimed at modifying a child's gender identity APA, 2021; Ashley, 2019b; Paré, 2020; SAMHSA, 2015; UN Human Rights Council, 2020), either covertly or overtly"* SOC 8.

If you don't question the source of this identity, you are treating a patient on the assumption of an accurate self-diagnosis. These children are now getting all the attention they crave. Their parents are suddenly actively involved in their lives, taking them for treatment and showing their concern. Online they have something new to talk about every day about their new discoveries as a trans, maybe go to an LGBTQI+ rally or a club meeting. They have become part of a self-perpetuating machine that churns through medications, damaged and discarded body parts and a ton of money. Upwards to 5 billion dollars a year.

Sincerity must be proven by any gender believer through sacrifice, and these undeveloped minds are ready to give it their all. The parents of trans, now social warriors with a noble cause to fight for, smile with pride. And for the unwary followers caught in this living machine by mistake or happenstance, a lifetime of regret for many. The movement plays down detransitioners and their numbers.

When a trans in congress was asked about detransitioners, he/she responded that they represent less than 1% of trans people and were not worth mentioning. How humorous, since trans at the time represented less than 1% of the general population, yet the 1% of detransitioners are not worthy of recognition in their own eyes. It's estimated that between 5 to 7 percent either detransition or revert to their birth sex before their transition is complete. They don't speak up or bring attention to themselves for fear of the wrath that will befall them. There also seems to be a pattern of molestation in trans males that eventually figure out on their own they wanted to be a man in response to their sexual abuse as a girl or woman. Since their reason for transition was never questioned, the real trauma was never addressed. Only after the additional trauma of transition did they realize gender affirmation was not a cure, just a band-aide. The progressive movement looks down on these damaged and scared detransitioners with disdain. Progressives hold society responsible for making them change back, along with lack of family support. There is little or no sympathy for the detransitioners or much medical assistance once initial transition is started.

It was not that long ago that a vast majority of the population set the bar for what counted as normal. The few that differed from the norm were designated as different or abnormal. The only way the few can establish dominance over the majority is to change the narrative. This is done by changing the terminology and establishing authority in doing so. Instead of normal or natural men and women, these terms were reassigned the new designation of Cis or Cisgender. The alternatives are transgender, nonbinary, gender fluid, gender noncongruent, and the list goes on. Progressives consistently claim more than 50 recognized gender roles.

Men and women haven't changed and neither have the male and female characteristics known as gender. To prove this hasn't changed, simply look at a trans man. In an ideal situation, they will have facial hair, no breasts, deep voice and dress as a truck driver, casual male or in a man's suite. They pursue the traditional appearance of masculinity as they perceive a man. A trans female will wear a dress or other traditional feminine attire, strive for a feminine figure, feminine voice, hairless face, make-up and hair style like a traditional woman. This is how they perceive it is to be a woman. Sex hasn't changed and neither has gender, only the narrative. All the other nuances such as non-binary, fluid etc. are simply cannon fodder to confuse the main issue.

Once a social movement has monopolized the terminology and the language, they get to write the rules. Being a woman becomes ambiguous with statements and catchphrases like "trans women are women". Now that this has been established as fact, it's time for the Cis population to recognize trans women as one and the same as natural women. Locker rooms, sororities, bathrooms, nothing is off limits to these guys with breasts (or without). They can leer at then expose themselves to women and young girls, then justify it by proclaiming they are trans.

The reality hasn't changed, but perception and interpretation have. Some states made it illegal to prevent trans men from violating women's spaces and some courts backed these laws. Let's look at an opposing California law that was never implemented or applied to trans people.

California Code, Penal Code - PEN § 314

Indecent Exposure

Every person who willfully and lewdly, either:

1. Exposes his person, or the private parts thereof, in any public place, or in any place where there are present other persons to be offended or annoyed thereby; or,

2. Procures, counsels, or assists any person so to expose himself or take part in any model artist exhibition, or to make any other exhibition of himself to public view, or the view of any number of persons, such as is offensive to decency, or is adapted to excite to vicious or lewd thoughts or acts, is guilty of a misdemeanor.

Every person who violates subdivision 1 of this section after having entered, without consent, an inhabited dwelling house, or trailer coach as defined in Section 635 of the Vehicle Code, or the inhabited portion of any other building, is punishable by imprisonment in the state prison, or in the county jail not exceeding one year.

Strange how no one ever used this law which is on the books in California. The simple presence of someone born male in a space reserved exclusively for women is disturbing to many women. It is a natural reaction comparable to dropping a mouse in a tank with a snake in it. When a trans woman (born male) decided to join a college sorority in Wyoming, six natural women members requested he leave. Born male at six foot two, 260 pounds he could be reasonably viewed as intimidating. These six members complained of visible erections through clothes, always having a pillow on his lap and other behavior they felt was unsettling. They were overridden by the sorority local chapters leadership which responded they do not discriminate against gender identity. Taking the matter to court, the judge found that sorority guidelines did not specifically define the term woman. Why would they ever feel the need to?

Since the rise of the identity movement the definition of a women has been debated in courts, congress and public opinion. This goes beyond the United States, but the origins of this movement are here in America. Let's get this straight once and for all what the definition of a woman is.

Woman Definition: A human born female with the natural potential to conceive, give birth to, and nurse a child.

Natural potential refers to women that may experience fertility problems, which makes them no less a woman. The natural potential is there, whereas a male is born without the essential anatomy to perform the above conditions. Natural procreation is a binary function no matter how much anyone dislikes the truth or facts. A woman with a beard is just a bearded lady, no matter what surgical procedures they have endured. A man with breasts reengineered medically will till his dying day remain a man that has been altered. Reality is not ambiguous, only opinion is.

Stigma is a frequently used word in the SOC in every version. One of WPATH's main missions is de-stigmatizing transsexualism through rebranding. Using phrases like archaic terminology and social bias, they have turned the linguistic tables by stigmatizing normal and natural. Relabeling sex at birth to assigned at birth, then giving an identity to those who accept the body they are born with as Cis or cisgender. Is it really a coincidence that the word cis can easily be associated with a hiss, the sound a snake makes. No, this is an intentional well-planned campaign to delegitimize normality. The word

Cis means cut in Latin, simplest example is scissors. Gender identity supporters insist it comes from Latin for near or same side as opposed to trans for travel. Another example is mathematical use, meaning same side of an axis. Nowhere outside of gender theory has Cis ever been associated with biology, anatomy, or sociology. If trans means travel than Cis means home?

Within the last decade, most of the world's population are expected to accept the label placed on them by a minority social movement. The term Cis is then used as a slur, the opposition, not one of us. The odd part of this is the compliance and complicitly of the LGB community, who are perfectly happy with the body they have. Cis in gender lingo refers to alignment with birth sex. This would mean LGB would classify as Cis! Why harmonize with transgender people, many of which view the LGB as closet trans that don't have the courage to be their true selves. To complicate sexual orientation further many trans insist they are straight while coupling with same birth sex partners.

If you read SOC version 8, you'll discover a very professional systematic approach to affirm (encourage), dislike of one's own body while completely absorbing them into a social belief system. This belief system is rebranded as support networking. Once indoctrinated, a series of treatments are scientifically applied under the umbrella of "medical necessity" to draw every dime they can from insurance companies and patients. This is not fixing any medical condition as much as creating one for profit. Some doctors participate in these treatments trusting the SOC guidelines with the best of intentions, only to be criticized and chastised by their peers when raising valid questions.

Apart from a few anomalies everyone is born either male or female. Those born with no or both sets of genitalia (intersex) have every right to follow the medical or social path they feel comfortable with. This is an instance where WPATH's guidelines and recommendations can correctly treat someone born with atypical genitalia. For a normal heathy well-defined adult, the option to identify as the opposite sex is a desire and choice that is not a medical necessity.

A medical necessity is when something is wrong in function or appearance that must be treated to achieve normalcy. Chemically or surgically altering a healthy and normal looking person is considered elective treatment which is not covered by insurance. Dysphoria which the SOC describes as a discomfort caused by incongruence or dissatisfaction with body appearance bypasses the elective element. Using the term "medical necessity", treatments like hair removal (including pubic), face and body sculpting along with multiple invasive and traumatic surgeries can be covered by some private insurance and Medicaid. Many normal woman and men suffer as much or more distress over their natural appearance or as they age.

Face lifts, liposuction and facial hair removal are not covered by insurance for normal people. These are basic procedures, not nearly as complicated or expensive as body and face sculpting. Were a psychiatrist to recommend such procedures as medically necessary for non-trans, they would never pass approval for insurance coverage. If any normal (Cis) person were to verbally consider suicide due to their appearance dysphoria, they'd be forcefully evaluated or committed until their distress dissipated.

It is possible for someone to live in two worlds at once. The real world that everyone shares and can observe through their senses, and the perceived world. In the perceived world every person interprets reality through a personal filter that buffers information in a more suitable format tailored to the individual. Familiarity and confirmation produce comfort, while conflict and trauma produce anxiety.

The best way to resolve anxiety is to address its source and take corrective action. This action must take place in the real world where everyone lives using the tools available. The alternatives are acceptance of conflict and trauma which can become internalized or escape from the issue at hand through fantasy. Escape through fantasy is never a safe course since it leaves you unprotected from reality, and it can become habitual. In the most extreme cases people can decide to become something they are not. This could be an animal, object or some historical figure.

Napoleon Bonapart is one such example. You can dress the part, learn French, demand to be called emperor while commanding an imaginary army, but it is living in fantasy. It doesn't require a degree in psychology to know this person needs to be brought back to reality and that affirming or encouraging his fantasy is not healthy. Telling everyone to go along and address him as emperor will end with him on horseback getting hit by a bus while leading a fantasy charge into battle.

The Napolean example is a parable. Reality must be delt with and accepted otherwise physical and/or further psychological damage will be the result. Illness of the mind has been around as long as people have existed. Analytical treatments and medications have advanced over the last 100 years all focused on the premise that some people need help accepting and dealing with reality. Some more than others.

In the most extreme cases being institutionalized is the only way to protect the individual or the public. Asylums continue to treat their patients with the hope that they may return to reality. Sometimes breakthroughs bring some back to the real world. The deeper the trauma along with the length of time spent avoiding reality, the more likely the chance a patient will regress. This happens when confronted with any number of triggers. Rather than reliving the pain of reality, the mind seeks comfort in the warm embrace of fantasy.

The younger someone is when trauma or a whim nudges them to choose fantasy over reality, the more likely they are to use this strategy as a form of self-defense. Children use their imagination to act out and gain perspective of the real world. Imagination is the mother of invention, but it can become a prison if reality becomes too frightening a place to live in. A human can't change their race, become a bird or a tree. By the same reasoning a man can't become a woman or a women become a man. Altering your appearance, voice and mannerisms can make a very convincing presentation. A trans convincing themselves that they are as they present are fooling themselves as much as anyone else. Maybe visiting an asylum and having a long talk with Napoleon would help put this in perspective for them.

Proper treatment for any disassociation from reality requires identification first. This means recognizing there is a problem, then through psychoanalysis identifying the cause. Next is treating the problem through therapy and sometimes medications. In an ideal situation the patient comes to accept and deal with reality in a productive way, relieving anxiety to a tolerable level. None of this process can occur without first recognizing there is a problem. For any professional in the medical field to claim transsexualism is a perfectly normal condition and not the cause or result of emotional distress to escape from reality is grossly negligent. Ignoring the high percentage of neurodiverse, mentally and emotionally afflicted members of the trans community is blatantly irresponsible.

It's far easier to blame society as a whole and human nature itself as the cause of gender dysphoria. How dare reality be so cruel to impose itself on anyone's fantasy. Transsexualism is a dissociative disorder by its own definition. You cannot treat any disorder if you refuse to recognize it. Rebranding this condition as gender incongruence puts the importance of gender identity above reality. Why encourage fantasy while diminishing the value of reality?

Here is another diagnosis with a relative description that WPATH either ignores or hasn't circumvented yet.

Symptoms of Body Dysmorphic Disorder:

People who have body dysmorphic disorder are preoccupied or obsessed with one or more perceived flaws in their appearance. This preoccupation or obsession typically focuses on one or more body areas or features, such as their skin, hair, or nose. However, "any body "area or part can be the subject of concern.

The Diagnostic & Statistical Manual of Mental Disorders, Fifth Edition (DSM-5) outlines the criteria for a diagnosis of body dysmorphic disorder.2 BDD is not classified as an eating disorder in the DSM-5. Instead, it is listed under the category of "Obsessive-Compulsive and Related Disorders." The DSM-5 lists the following diagnostic criteria:

- Preoccupation with one or more perceived defects in appearance that are not noticeable to others and are not truly disfigured.
- At some point, the person suffering has performed repetitive actions or thoughts in response to the concerns. This may be something like continuously comparing their appearance to that of others, mirror checking, or skin picking.
- This obsession causes distress and problems in a person's social, work, or other areas of life.

This obsession isn't better explained as a symptom of an eating disorder (although some people may be diagnosed with both).

Now this confirmed mental disorder directly describes transsexualism and gender dysphoria. Genitalia and secondary sexual characteristics are the perceived flaws that trans people fixate and stress over. How can anyone validate one description as a mental disorder while dismissing the big dysphoric elephant in the room?

This is not a situation where no harm is inflicted on children. Many of these recommendations in the SOC involve medical interventions with no long-term studies. Gender fluid means a child could change their gender as often as the weather. The irreversible or somewhat reversible effects of some gender affirming care cannot keep up with a child's fickle nature. Using six months of consistent atypical behavior is no reason to interfere in the natural growth and emotional development of any child. Encouraging this behavior through gender affirming psychotherapy is an imbalanced approach that promotes a predetermined outcome. Affirmation therapy is the opposite of reparative. There are many stories about successful reparative therapy online and I have included one I found very informative below.

"Having adopted a transgender identity as a child, I am familiar with the feelings of self-loathing, the desire to kill myself and become someone new, as well as the intense difficulty in feeling connected to my body. To say I felt like I was in the wrong body is an understatement. I remember watching science fiction shows where scientists had created the technology to move someone's brain into a new body and longed to not only be in a different body, but in a different time when that technology was available.

In my case, I developed the identity of Timothy. Timothy was strong and mean. And most importantly, as a boy, he would not fall victim to the violations that men perpetrated on Erin. This identity helped me navigate some other difficulties in my life as well. Ever since my parents divorced, my mother told me that my biological father wanted me to be a boy. I believed that my dad would love Timothy in a way he didn't love Erin. I also had a serious learning disability. Girls were supposed to read well, but the expectations were lower for boys. It was okay that Timothy struggled to decipher the meaning of letters on a page. I was quirky and hadn't fit in with the other girls who seemed to naturally navigate social situations. As a boy, I could play rough and tumble, rather than socializing with the girls.

Erin Brewer, MS. Ph.D.

To read more or other links go to:

I recommend the letter to school counselor link, it's very informative to parents.

This is a story from someone that has experienced what many confused and traumatized children go through. Fortunately, the author went to real psychotherapists not tainted by WPATHs' belief system. The SOC guidelines encourage treating the imaginary identity rather than identify the underlying true cause of distress. A gender therapist is never supposed to question a child's self-proclaimed gender identity, only assist and insist on their transition in every possible way. Treating the symptoms and ignoring the illness is not good medicine; it does not benefit the patient. To throw your hands up and scientifically proclaim any common illness is completely incurable is not acceptable in any other circumstance. There will always be a few incurable cases, but chemical alteration and surgical manipulation should not be prescribed like aspirin to children.

The original SOC insisted on thorough psychological testing and evaluation before any gender affirming therapy. The current SOC version 8 places the patients' self-diagnosis as a responsible indicator to focus on transition first and therapy later.

Besides affirming incongruent behavior in children, the family and friends of every trans initiate must become a warrior like advocate. Those with no trans or non-binary relative can contribute by becoming an ally. Many people have little reason to exist outside of latching onto a cause or some other form of ideal to give their life meaning. The typical human passions normally suppressed are encouraged by radical elements in every movement. This includes politics, religion, or social belief systems. Hive or mob mentality happens when enough people of like minds gather in person or online. People lose their sense of personal responsibility by riding the wave of emotion that forms when groups focus on a single cause or object.

Opposing forces are the easiest points of focus since any adversary is a threat that triggers the flight or fight response. The progressive movement is one such wave ready to rally its warriors and allies at any sign of adversity. WPATH is and could be so beneficial to people born intersex or with other sexual and genetic anomalies. They now choose instead to serve as the spearhead of a movement that has become cult like with political power. They are an organization that advocates castrating adolescent boys and men that wish to become eunuchs. How can that be justified as medically necessary or innate?

Damage Report

We know about the physical damage caused by transition, now let's discuss the psychological, social and indirect results of progressive philosophy. Living in a fantasy world leaves any individual vulnerable to the dangers that exist in reality. Believing you can fly will result in broken bones or death. Believing you are a man when you have a functional female reproductive system can result in pregnancy. Being alone in the wrong place can result in an altercation. Being different or out of place can put a target on your back in some social situations. For anyone to believe they are impervious to these facts of reality is dangerous. The laws against hate crimes have brought the frequency of incidents down a little, but in most instances their effect on outcomes is minor at best. Any group of people of like minds will respond to and focus their ire on someone that is different.

The progressive solution to this human response is forced compliance and indoctrination. This is better known as safety in numbers. Forcing schools to form a safety net around trans students along with a supportive family unit can create a limited safe space where an odd child displaying an alternate gender identity can dwell. Punishing classmates for not using pronouns or alternative names only breeds contempt and resentment in most minds. Bathrooms, locker rooms, athletic fields and hallways are not so safe. Now the trans student must rush from one safe place to the next or gather in small groups for short journeys. A trans female doesn't use the girl's bathroom and locker rooms to feel more female, they do it more out of fear or entitlement. Kids can be cruel, so why create this situation to promote a social statement? Girls and women shouldn't need to sacrifice their safe places to placate some confused male's identity.

Gender identity is a limited social construct, not a valid physical reason to impose on someone else's personal rights or sense of safety. A trans female in a California high school made a public statement that he carried a knife and would stab any female that complains about his presence in a girl's bathroom. If he's so tough in a dress and armed with a knife, why is he so determined not to use the boy's bathroom? It is a prime example of a man asserting his authority over women to prioritize his personal beliefs.

Progressives and the alphabet gang have imposed the title of privileged among its members while claiming fragility and persecution. Giving any segment of society special privileges and protections can only result in the loss of the same protection to someone else. That is the very definition of privilege. If you want to express your identity through gender rather than deeds, then go for it. No one else needs to suffer or change because of your choices.

Gender identity and expression is a conscious choice, not an uncontrollable force that cannot be resisted, otherwise how can it also be fluid? Don't fluid choices equate to whimsical? Trends have changed throughout recent history, from the beat nicks to the hippies with long hair, jocks, ra-ra's, stoners, bikers, goth, and currently, gender identity. Until the last few decades, the medical community considered breast augmentation before the age of 18 unethical, because growth hasn't completed, making alterations unstable. Now they're promoting amputating breasts of 16-year-olds under their own guidelines while claiming medical necessity. This is a professional-backed social club that sells privilege. But privilege has its price.

In Oklahoma a high school sophomore girl that identified as they/them was in the girl's bathroom when three freshman girls made comments about her clothes and laughter. She threw water on the three freshmen girls, and a fight started. The friend she was with ran away, but the fight ended quickly when the older girl hit the floor. She was taken to a hospital and released home. She had escalated the incident to a physical altercation and her friends stated later that she was aggressive about her identity. Abandoned by her parents, raised by her grandma and not from an affluent background, her social identity was all she had. The next morning, she was found dead in her room. News channels across the country reported that most likely striking her head during the struggle was the cause of death. Adding that the hospital was at fault and the three girls she confronted should be locked up and charged with murder.

The alphabet mob was furious and out for blood. When the autopsy confirmed she had overdosed on her antidepressants it was met with doubt and more calls to charge the three girls. Long dissertations, properly using they/them pronouns which were almost impossible to read, complained about publicly using her dead name (birth name) instead of her new gender name. The alphabet activists took to the streets demanding justice for their new martyr while the three other girls from the altercation were driven into hiding. Candles were lit and vigils held while activist lawyers descended on her grandma's house. This kind of attention was the very reason that girl took her own life.

All that girl needed was a good therapist to tell her that life had more importance than an alternate identity. Things would eventually get better for her if she just hung in there and believed in herself. Sometime during her last night, she must have realized just how lonely and scared she really was and that a social identity was not the answer she needed. The only community she knew was expecting so much from her, but they were also the cause of her dilemma. She could only think of one way out, and a teenage girl died alone by her own hand.

Looking for fault, the progressive activists accused the school's bathroom code of causing her death along with lack of security. Unisex bathrooms would have had no different outcome, and you can't post security in every bathroom. The twisted part of this story is that in the end her gender identity had more value than her life.

A popular show televised on a cable network tells the story of a teen-age drug addict and her trans friend amongst other characters. Social media lit up with various opinions and theories about the trans female character which catapulted the show into success. One of the early episodes include the trans female teenager having sex with a man in his forties. Although the teens' implied age in the show is 17, there is no indication of how long this had been going on. This was celebrated in the trans community as a trans journey of self-discovery, but in the real world the outcome can vary.

Such is the case of a 14-year-old trans girl that rendezvoused with a 29-year-old man at three in the morning in a small town in Pennsylvania. This kid's family fully supported the male to female transition. As a modern progressive family, they dove into the world of gender identity and networked with local organizations of like mind. From all the descriptions this teen trans girl was happy, joyful, and well balanced. Lighting up every room with her trans presence, culminating in the picture-perfect model of everything the SOC and trans community hope to aspire to. One night she left a friend's house to meet up with a grown man she located on a same sex for sex dating app. By three in the morning her phone was turned off, and some time afterward a few of her body parts were discovered in a local park. They had a suspect in custody before most of her body could be recovered.

The family contacted the local trans support groups which organized a vigil proclaiming the deceased's preferred pronouns which are respected here. Any child's death is tragic, a young life ending like this is nothing short of horrific. What is odd is that no one questions the events leading up to this crime. Why is any young teen seeking out adult sex partners? Possibly the same reason many abused women are attracted to abusers, to relive a trauma experienced when they were young. Women sexually abused by older men when very young tend to be attracted to older or powerful men that they identify with their abuser.

Very young boys that are sexually abused may be sexually stimulated at the time but can't process what is happening to them. This becomes a traumatic focal point in their lives that they can't assimilate so they react with a child's reasoning. It would not have happened if they were a girl, since their abuser liked boys. The same way some trans boys switch genders in response to abuse happening because they were born female. In a child's mind they are making themselves unattractive to their abusers they have no other defense against. Was this 14-

year-old a victim of sexual abuse that responded by wishing to be a female? Did he then go on to relive the abuse at the hands of an older male? We will never know since his life was cut short. It is much easier to declare transsexualism is innate and should never be questioned than treat a troubled mind. How many lives could be saved with the correct reparative therapy?

Now some may argue that this is faulty theory with no evidence-based truth to it. But I can truthfully say I have personally witnessed this behavior far too many times for it to be coincidence. Here is a common example everyone can understand. Most humans have experienced sexual stimulation or an orgasm. The very first time you experienced this was a traumatic moment in your life. When your body physically responded beyond your control for the first time it was both frightening and exciting. It wasn't long afterward that you wanted to relive that moment, like the phrase," feels like the first time". For those that were terrified by the experience or fearful of their first experience, a sense of dread can occur. Fearing that it could happen again or at all may result in people refusing to accept their genitalia or desperately wishing to disable the possibility through surgical or chemical means. Becoming a eunuch for example.

If the first-time trauma of orgasm or sexual stimulation is tied to a forced or abusive moment the mind will either reject or embrace it, but this trauma never goes unanswered. The mind must address the issue and create a response to deal with the anxiety of the moment. Creating a new view of life or another identity are two such responses to this kind of trauma. Both processes are self-defense mechanisms that either ignore or rationalize the bad memory so life can go on. Once the initial trauma is delt with, the memory is buried in a safe place to prevent the emotional pain from surfacing. Problem is, it is a part of you that never goes away and some of it will seep into everyday mental processes.

Asking a patient why they dislike the reality of their birth sex, or why it causes them so much anxiety could reveal a significant trauma that can be addressed. This would involve accepting that there is a problem and identifying the problem. Proper therapy could then work to free a tortured mind from a life of misery. These logical paths of thought contradict the established beliefs of WPATH and the SOC, that transsexualism is innate and a perfectly natural and healthy frame of mind. Imagine all those damaged minds at WPATH hiding behind their subconscious self-defense mechanisms, whimsical theories and body altering disguises. It's quite disturbing to view this social movement and their army of credentialed professionals as a structured organization based on denial. Envision a self-perpetuating entity created from so many damaged parts feeding on itself and anything it touches. Dante would be inspired.

Dr Cass pointed out in her report that there is no single explanation for the current trend to seek transition or break away from traditional gender roles. Children today are exposed to opinions, ideas and pornography that they did not have easy access to until two decades ago. Children gather around smart phones in school yards and lunchrooms sharing content that corrupts the innocence of childhood. Currently this raw data is consumed and shared by young minds in early elementary school. When young children are subjected to sexual trauma, they tend to mature sooner than their peers.

This is caused by having to deal with adult issues before their age group normally must.

The days of magazines displaying bare breasts and airbrushed lower extremities are long gone, replaced by blatant sexual activity many adults would be shocked by. Pair this with the parallel content found in modern cartoons and web channels that exhibit adult themes with children presented as mature and knowledgeable in adult matters. How are we not surprised by the resulting gender identity chaos we find so hard to comprehend? The older generations have no personal experience to compare modern childhood to.

It cannot be a coincidence that as much as 80% of trans exhibit autism and/or moderate psychological and/or emotional issues such as depression, loneliness and PTSD. It is a certainty that not every child seeking transition has been sexually molested though some have. One fact that no one can deny is children are still children. They lack the life experience of an adult that has gone through puberty, adolescence, working, paying bills and shouldering responsibility. Watching porn and mimicking adult behavior does not make them mature enough to make a medical decision that can or will damage them for the rest of their lives. They do not have a true concept of time or the attention span of their grandparents. They are consumed by desire to assume an identity that appeals to them and their friends. If their parents give them attention because of this identity, great, if it has a negative result, at least they'll get noticed. Children already have enough bad impulses and ideas without the medical community encouraging them to demand medical intervention.

There was a video with two siblings ages eight and five declaring they couldn't wait to be old enough to go on puberty blockers as if it were some rites of passage. Children this age shouldn't be aware of these matters, nor should they feel the need to pick a gender identity. The odd part was the father displaying his pride in their enthusiasm. A mature sound mind does not risk their child's health to be popular on social media or social networks. Many parents introduce these concepts to their children intentionally to promote the progressive message and become part of the new social revolution.

Before the internet changed everyone's social structure, children would learn through interaction with each other. Any information consumed came from personal contact, radio, television, parents, and school. In the late sixties through late seventies neighborhoods were packed with kids of all age groups. Kids sorted themselves by their age and sex. Boys did boy things and girls did their things with others of their own age group. Male and female didn't socially mix until puberty when hormones and information from older siblings and friends raised curiosity about the opposite sex. Mothers would teach their daughters early about sex for their own protection while boys were left mostly to their own devises until sex education in junior high school.

Children born after 1963 altered this dynamic. Boys and girls born in 1964 and later played with and befriended each other as equals. Children born before this time would tease anyone having a friend of the opposite sex before puberty as having a boyfriend or girlfriend. The immediate response would be denial and that they were just talking. Similar separation of the sexes would continue through high school and adulthood at gatherings where the couples would break off into separate groups of male or female. This new generation ended that tradition. They may have been the earliest noticeable step in social evolution in the U.S.

Before the seventies it was not uncommon to go through school without sharing a classroom with other races. Forced integration caused a cultural shock when black and white students were suddenly thrust together in classrooms. Each race would eye the other with suspicion and curiosity. Many of these kids only knowledge of each other was what they'd heard from their parents or siblings. Clothing, slang, behavior, even body language was reason enough for conflict which sometimes escalated into fights or school skirmishes. It took a few decades for everyone to work out their differences although there still exists some small contention to this day. At the time of integration, few special protections were enforced for either race, they let the kids work it out.

We have a similar cultural shift now with the gender identity issue. A small but fair percentage of the population have joined a movement that is in direct contradiction to the long-standing status quo. An established acceptance that you are what you were born, to state otherwise is a state of mind, not an established fact.

Girls' sports and private areas are separated for a biological reason and should be respected as theirs and theirs alone. The qualifications for being a woman are set at birth and not in a gender clinic. No one born male has any business in a girl's bathroom, locker room or competing with or against females unless it is coed. If you are a male that wants to express your feminine side, then do so at your own risk, not at the expense of others. The reality everyone else lives in will not change for you or your fantasy. If you can show your face in class wearing a dress, then wear it in the boy's bathroom or an alternative bathroom for the shy or gender conflicted.

Women and girls need their special place to feel safe just as much as trans demand safety while taking away that right from women. Nothing a trans female may think or believe gives them the right to deny real women their birthright. There is a big difference between rights and privilege. Privilege denies the rights of others.

Trans people tend to feel persecuted, and in many respects they are. For the most part they are bullied by everyone from family to past friends, and any stranger seeking to project cruelty. The same thing happened in the early sixties with long hair, the nerds, black activists, pacifists and other cultural renegades. If you want to be different from everyone else and represent a social statement you will get responses to that statement you don't like.

One popular trans activist born male stated he was a girl at the age of five. His parents didn't explain to their boy he could never be a real girl or the severe pain and hardship he would suffer to disguise himself as one. They took him to a gender clinic instead. Somehow this story went viral, and the parents profited by portraying the systematic transition of a male to a female beginning at the age of six and continuing into adulthood. To complete the process his male parts were removed and an artificial vagina was installed, followed by a few serious infections.

Artificial body alterations can have severe complications. The doctor performing the surgeries was the best in the business, until she publicly stated children shouldn't surgically transition. WPATH responded by hiring the doctor as upper management and the large paycheck altered her opinion on the matter.

The child is now an adult cashing in on speaking engagements while complaining about why her children's book encouraging transition has been banned. No longer a functional male, she needs hormones the rest of her life which also make her gain weight. There's a good chance she'd never experienced a normal male orgasm; the possibility was chemically canceled at a young age for all to see on her show. She can never experience a female orgasm either. Nobody of sound mind loses a healthy body part with indifference or joy. No medical professional should encourage such behavior either. When a five-year-old makes an uninformed statement, you don't plan their whole life around their uneducated childish misconception of reality. The SOC says to do just that, never question, always affirm.

Politics

At a hearing a progressive agent claimed barring trans women from women's sports was the equivalent of barring black women from white women's bathrooms in the sixties. Statements like these confirm the instability of their argument. The biological differences between the sexes are as obvious today as they were then. The only similarity is the imposition of privilege by one group or race over another. This is the same form of privilege the trans community is demanding to impose, their rights over the rights of others. Equal rights infer that everyone abides by the same rules with no individual or group having exclusion from these same rules. Everyone has a designated sex at birth; call it assigned if you want but everyone has a physical description that falls into the binary of male or female. Only people born intersexed have any valid argument on this point.

Every American has a legal right to change their name to anything they like. Until your name is changed legally you are identified by your birth name. Traditional names consist of a surname, forename and optional middle name. The surname or family name is the last name used when signing documents. Most commonly the last name is associated with the father of the offspring they are responsible for. The first name is the individual identifier which often reflects a child's gender or birth sex, though some names may be used for either sex. Your name is your identity both legally and socially. Nicknames are normally descriptive alternate identifiers applied by family, friends or associates. They are not legal without an official name change, though sometimes added on documents as AKA (also known as). It is common for entertainers and other high-profile people to create a single name or phrase to represent themselves as a brand unique to themselves.

In this new digital age of social media children and adults create an odd identifier to attract attention then work on content to grow a following. These people search social networks to see what works for the more successful influencers, then target a group they feel they can attract. Foodies, travelers, style, gardening and the trans community. There's good money to be made by the savvy child that wishes to become famous with no regard for what it may do to their health. Parents wishing to make a living off their child's identity will sometimes push or create gender incongruence for profit driven reasons or fame.

Anytime you see a very young child imitating the opposite sex you'll notice the proud parent nearby with a big smile ready to give an interview about how proud they are to assist their child's transition. Someone had to buy the clothes and sign the papers for gender treatment. Many parents leap at the opportunity to encourage transition to become part of a community that gives their life value and meaning. This pattern is similar to child beauty pageant moms that live their lives through their children's modeling, giving their own existence meaning.

When a child makes a remark that they do not associate with their body the parent should attempt to reason with their child and find out where this idea came from. If that doesn't work, take them to a real child psychologist or psychiatrist that can perform an intensive evaluation. This will reveal if there is a spectrum element that needs to be addressed along with a profile that may quickly expose the cause of their gender incongruence. Therapy will then help them accept the reality of their physical body. The child may still wish to be the opposite sex, but they bond with their physical body with an absence of dysphoria because they accepted reality.

Take this same child to a gender specialist that follows the SOC, and within a few hours gender incongruence, with signs of dysphoria will likely be diagnosed. If the parent says this has been going on for six months or more the treatment waiting period is waived, and affirmation therapy can be initiated. This involves different hair, clothes, and most importantly a new name and pronouns. Affirmation takes precedence over all and any other spectrum, mental or emotional disorders.

SOC 8 page s63 list of recommendations.

Mental health difficulties may challenge the assessment and treatment of gender-related needs of TGD adolescents in various ways: 1. First, when a TGD adolescent is experiencing acute suicidality, self-harm, eating disorders, or other mental health crises that threaten physical health, safety must be prioritized. According to the local context and existing guidelines, appropriate care should seek to mitigate the threat or crisis so there is sufficient time and stabilization for thoughtful gender-related assessment and decision-making. For example, an actively suicidal adolescent may not be emotionally able to make an informed decision regarding gender-affirming medical/surgical treatment.

"If indicated, safety-related interventions should not preclude starting gender-affirming care."

2. Second, mental health can also complicate the assessment of gender development and gender identity-related needs. For example, it is critical to differentiate gender incongruence from specific mental health presentations, such as obsessions and compulsions, special interests in autism, rigid thinking, broader identity problems, parent/child interaction difficulties, severe developmental anxieties (e.g., fear of growing up and pubertal changes unrelated to gender identity), trauma, or psychotic thoughts. Mental health challenges that interfere with the clarity of identity development and gender-related decision-making should be prioritized and addressed.

S48 6.5- We recommend against offering reparative and conversion therapy aimed at trying to change a person's gender and lived gender expression to become more congruent with the sex assigned at birth.

Looking at the excerpts, it seems that WPATH is very aware that many factors cause behavior that may culminate in a misdiagnosis. An intensive evaluation that tests for learning disabilities with a full psychological profile involves 16 or more hours of tests and another 3-5 weeks of evaluating the results to produce a comprehensive report. Complications such as spectrum issues or gender incongruence could require additional time and evaluation. These profiles should be required before anything as drastic as chemical, surgical, or affirmation therapy are recommended. Getting in to see a top-notch psychological practitioner can take months and without insurance can cost upwards of several thousand dollars or more. Without first addressing all the elements pertaining to behavior an accurate assessment of gender incongruence cannot be performed.

Gender clinics across the country have opened their doors with nurse practitioners and licensed counselors making medical evaluations and decisions they are not qualified to perform according to the SOC. They are the gender equivalent to opioid pill factories that cause so much harm in our society. Without a professional and comprehensive evaluation as indicated by the SOC in the above excerpt, the issue of transsexualism cannot begin to be addressed.

Obsession is very common in the atypical behavior exhibited in autism. If gender identity is the object of that obsession feeding into the obsession is no different than giving an alcoholic a case of liquor. Telling a confused patient longing for an answer to their distress that they are incurable from birth (innate), or in the wrong body is nurturing fantasy. Misdirecting the emotionally or mentally impaired to align with their fantasy is causing harm.

Declassifying gender incongruence as a mental illness is a misnomer. The word gender, once used to represent the social expectations of behavior parallel with sex has morphed into everyone's own interpretation. The correct terminology should be sexual incongruence which is a specific form of body dissociation. Dissociation is currently listed as a mental illness. Put it all together and you can plainly see that people that ignore or refuse to accept physical reality display symptoms of mental illness.

Gender has been successfully nullified as a definitive word by a social movement attempting to control the narrative. Gender has evolved into its own entity, entirely separate from and unassociated with sex. This was intentionally planned and well implemented by progressives. Try as they might to claim sex is not binary, for procreation it still takes a man and a woman to reproduce in nature. Intersex or people devoid of sex organs have birth defects no different from people born with missing /deformed limbs or mental impairment. There is no shame in this, and it makes them no less human. We don't describe them as different types of humans, simply people with imperfections. To claim the word defect has a stigma to it is the act of stigmatizing a noun that has been used in every language for thousands of years. Anyone so fragile or sensitive to the word defective, a noun that means flawed, should learn how to face reality.

Some people that experience mental illness will never be cured. In the old days they were labeled as mad or insane. Which brings us back to the dozens of Napoleons that are alive and well living in modern times. To say they are not mentally ill because mental illness has a stigma (negative connotation) does not negate their mental condition. Telling everybody to use the pronouns Emperor or General around him and reinforce his fantasy as innate behavior will not bode well with many. It is the essence of an abnormal identity, one that is not common or based in reality. The trans movement is no different, you can declassify it as a sign of mental illness, force pronoun use, promote acceptance through education and laws, but it doesn't change reality. The stigma may diminish but it will never go away, the perception of abnormality is all too apparent to a reasonable mind that lives in the real world.

There are some transexual people that are unreachable. They believe they are the opposite of their birth sex despite, or in denial of their physical body. They refuse to accept the reality of their birth sex in the real world while living in an alternate fantasy. These are the rare and few incurable types of patients the founders of WPATH originally studied and gave up on.

They just threw their hands up and said they can't find the cause of this illness so it must be innate and incurable. This happened over 60 years ago and no one at WPATH has ever questioned the validity of these findings. They would rather misrepresent studies and promote theories that reinforce one man's misguided and archaic conclusions. You can never find the solution to any problem if the fundamental elements are incorrect.

By natural design men and women are different, one of each are required to reproduce. For purposes of reproduction sex is only binary, sexual birth defects are just that, imperfect reproductive organs. The woman's body is designed to feed the newborn whereas the male body has no such biological capacity. Men and women have different primary steroid production which tend to induce nurturing in women and aggression in men. These biological differences have resulted in different behaviors particular to each sex forming the binary gender categories of feminine and masculine. Though either sex may display periodic actions attributed the opposite sex, such as an aggressive woman or an empathetic male. Generalized behavior attributed to each sex in a social situation resulted in the descriptive term gender.

Gender was directly associated with sex and in many instances the terms were used interchangeably since gender had a softer appeal as opposed to the more medical term sex. Men were expected to be aggressive, combative and competitive, while women were nurturing, amiable, and groomed to be attractive. Subdivisions developed between the two genders such as the terms ladies and gentlemen, which elevated masculine and feminine to a more refined and civilized set of rules and expectations. The wealthier or more powerful the better educated, dressed and bejeweled the individual genders became with each step up leading them further away from their animal origins. From the Kings court down to the lowliest servant, gender prevailed through the ages as an identity and a social response to the need for survival.

The more we conquered our environment the less need we had for these very instincts to survive. Power and wealth became trophies as the traditional family unit disintegrated and fell by the wayside. More parents left their families out of boredom or for personal advantage with little thought given to parental responsibility or concern about how their offspring would survive. Having children, which once meant leaving a legacy and a future for the human race were put on the back burner while financials and careers were prioritized.

Calculators once banned in schools in the mid-seventies became as common as pencils replacing the need to learn basic mathematics. Paper was replaced by a keyboard as cursive writing and penmanship disappeared along with the logical paths of thought created by basic math memorization. Physical education disappeared in many schools because the unhealthy kids felt left out and complained rather than participate in the very thing they needed. Before the mid-eighties, kids were forced to participate in P.E. and got healthier from it. Helicopter parents now drop their kids off and pick them up from school, so they don't have to walk any more than necessary.

Gone are the days of walking or riding a bike to school with your friends and making plans for the afternoon. For the last twenty years many children's thumbs do all the work while they stare into a screen sunup to sundown sharing texts and links, while never bothering to use their phone to speak to their friends. Direct social interaction has deteriorated as well as the ability to effectively communicate verbally.

The body does not develop as efficiently without physical exercise. Running, using all your muscles and coordination releases adrenalin and countless other hormones that balance body chemistry. Activity and exertion make the body sweat, flushing the pores and releasing toxins that have direct influence on brain function. Take any depressed kid and have them run a mile, then ask them if they feel better. Make them do it every day increasing the distance, along with bike riding or swimming a few days a week, this will improve their physical and mental health. Some high schoolers have started visiting the gym, not to be cool, but to feel better physically and mentally.

Many children's only exercise is walking from one classroom to another. All their energy is spent staring at their phones 8 or more hours a day, they've never read a book or verbally debated with others. These kids have no future plans and no interactive life experience outside of lunch or between classes at school. They've been exposed to porn since grade school, are second generation devoid of survival instinct or instruction and unable to process reality because they don't live in it. The algorithms have been feeding them nonsense, which they believe is real.

As an example, a few Years ago, a man in Miami consumed bath salts, hallucinated, and had partially eaten another man's face. This was a horrendous story. Many of the kids on the internet promoted and believed that the walking dead show had become real. Panic and fear were widespread, enough to be considered a mental crisis. Take the same gullible kids and convince them that gender has no relevance or structure and that all masculinity is toxic. Include the parents that are consuming the same information, it doesn't take much imagination to see how we got to where we are.

Many countries have stopped supporting WPATH's beliefs after having performed their own independent studies. England had the most comprehensive review while most Nordic countries once spearheading the charge to gender enlightenment have now reversed course also. Outside the U.S it has become apparent that the benefits of gender therapy do not outweigh the damage. Canada is still supportive, but the main influence of gender and trans theory mainly lies here in the states where it all started. This social movement which imbedded itself in the Democratic party contributed to that party's loss in the presidential election. Many Democrats and Independents couldn't stomach the progressives' radical elements invasiveness and chose not to vote or switched sides. The conservative administration is not supportive of the gender movement and sees this medical farce for what it is. They have no need for the gender movement's vote or influence.

The conservative movement has its own radical element based on tradition and religion. The Old Testament was written by and for the Jewish nation when it was a nomadic horde which roamed the desert conquering other nations. These same desert landscapes were known to swallow up whole armies up until the late 20th century. It was a harsh life, and the people had to work as one united force. They were among the first to set down in writing a moral code called the ten commandments claiming that God guided the hand that wrote them. These rules were delivered after Moses led his people away from Egypt and into the desert.

The people had fallen into an immoral rabble, turning on each other to take what little their neighbors had. Moses laid down the new laws and declared anyone not willing to live by them would be left behind. The Jewish nation split into two groups and the group that turned their backs on God's new laws were swallowed up by the desert. That doesn't mean the ground opened up and consumed them. It means they perished without the morals and laws needed by a mass of people in a harsh environment.

The Jewish nation at the time was warlike and couldn't function without strict discipline. Their beliefs and traditions were instilled in their children, not unlike how they are today. Their stories are celebrated on high holidays; reliving tales of how their beliefs have provided their survival. It must be true to some degree; they are the only nation that has lasted nearly four thousand years. A Rabbi named Jesus came along and started his own sect, preaching peace and harmony but most importantly passivity. After his death the Romans adopted the Christian religion to rein in their restless citizens and sooth their discontent. Assembling the first four recognized accounts of his life, they formed the early Roman Catholic Church. The Greek Orthodox adopted a similar version. A standardized version of the bible was produced in English in 1611 known as the King James version. This was written for the common people who did not speak or understand Latin or Greek.

The Pilgrims were puritans, the British, Protestants, Irish and Italians catholic. America is a melting pot not only of different nations but of different religions mostly Christian based. All

Christian sects believe in a moral code and a structured family unit that echoes the Hebraic and Christian model. In the 1950's most religious people viewed politics as a filthy business best to be avoided. This changed in the 60's as religious groups began jockeying for a stronger voice in American government. Latching onto the Republican party they amassed significant power promoting laws reflecting morals more aligned with Christian beliefs.

This is exactly how the LGBTQ movement usurped the Democratic party as a valuable voting bloc. This does not mean Democrats (liberals) are not people of faith. Liberals are more prone to accept nontraditional people or beliefs. As opposed to the conservatives that have little tolerance for progressive or liberal thoughts and actions. In the new digital age people have been manipulated through algorithms and news channels to believe they must pick a side. Which is true if you register to vote. Your options for registration are Democrat, Republican or Independent. Radical elements on both sides have divided the country in two, teaching hatred and mistrust of the other side. This leaves the independents and moderates from both parties stuck in the middle, refusing to fall into the mob mentality of either side. The result is the current American demographics of one third right, one third left, and the rest in the middle.

The right, most moderates, and many of the left view the gender movement as a passing fad and a social threat damaging children. The many trans laws both proposed and passed have focused on prohibiting the medical community from harming children. Without intensive testing and evaluation, no gender therapy should ever be mentioned or offered to a child by a healthcare professional. Nor should this take place in any of the "one day on your way" gender clinics that have spread throughout the country. Many of these businesses are staffed by people that believe they are helping children get what they need, having fallen into the gender theory mindset. An alcoholic needs a drink, or an addict needs a drug, while the gender confused need to become someone else. All these conditions are wants, and a means to escape the pain of reality. They are not needs, medical necessities or in the best interests of the afflicted.

Only by facing and accepting reality can you defeat dysphoria, anything else is feeding a fantasy. When a patient is ill, the doctor informs them what the problem is and the options to correct it. They do not ignore the illness, recommend medications that alter the body's functions and tell them changing their clothes and name will fix everything. That is treating disillusionment with more illusion, no different from the doctors that performed lobotomies to relieve dysphoria with similar negative side effects.

Part of the identity transition involves changing your name. Many trans or gender fluid and non-binary have been told or decided that you cannot fully become someone else until legally changing your name. Every adult has this right to change their legal name or that of their children. For the gender challenged this has become a rite of passage that reportedly brings them great euphoria, the opposite of dysphoria. For some this is not enough, they feel the need to change their sex on their personal ID and legal documents. This creates a problem since you cannot change your sex, only your appearance.

Many trans feel it gives them special status that overrides the rights of others that follow proper etiquette in respect to sexually segregated privacy. Bathrooms, locker rooms and women's competition are suddenly a target that trans and their alphabet mob feel the need to challenge. The gender confused point at their altered driver's license claiming they have every right to ignore societies division of the sexes that ensures fairness and privacy.

Women have a different body than men, designed by nature to perform different duties. These differences grace women with the advantage when it comes to acrobatics, ballet, and other activities where precision and grace are needed. Whereas men have more advantage with their brute strength, longer stride, larger lungs and muscle mass. In running and swimming competitions men have a natural advantage since strength and size affect how quickly they can run or swim. A man could fare poorly in competition with other men and proclaim they are trans to compete against women where they can use their natural advantage.

An army of radicals claim there are no advantages for biological males in women's competitions. It does not take a genius to see in the track winners circle that trans women have dominated their biological female competitors. If your competition is 1-2 feet taller with a 20% longer stride, that is an advantage. Women military recruits suffer twice the skeletal and joint injuries marching at male rates carrying weight. Any true athlete has sacrificed their childhood, social life, their bodies and their time to become the best they can be. The Williams sisters are a prime example of this sacrifice, training their entire lives to become the best. You don't see trans women competing on the balance beam or uneven bars where women's finesse and grace matter. No, they want to compete where they have the physical advantage that comes with having a man's biology.

Some folks have tried bending the rules claiming biological males that take steroids to suppress testosterone should be allowed to compete with women. Do steroids shrink lung capacity or shorten their legs and muscles? And what about trans men that take testosterone giving them more strength and muscle. They can't compete against other girls and women since steroid use is not permitted in scholastic or professional competitions. You are an athlete or a trans, you cannot be both unless competing only against your birth sex, other trans people or in designated co ed events.

Women's sports are for women, adding the trans prefix means they are not true women that can fairly compete. If you really wanted to be an athlete, you would sacrifice like all real athletes do. Delay your social identity or put it off until your athletic career is over, then train the body you are born with to compete fairly with others of the same birth sex. Anyone agreeing with these thoughts is instantly labeled a transphobe or a hater. It is not hateful to state the obvious. Living in reality and using common sense are virtues that the gender incongruent refuse to accept or recognize. They demand everyone view the world through their eyes, living in the fantasy they've created. Everything to their advantage is good and just while everyone else is antagonist that must change to suit their needs, wants and desires.

School text and library books should not contain sexually explicit content in elementary or middle schools. Starting in late middle school, literature should be provided for sex education that focuses on the mechanics of human sexual reproduction, STD's and birth control. High school students are mature enough to process the multiple social issues affecting our world. They are approaching adulthood and should be well informed of the different possibilities open to them as they deal with reality. Teaching a variety of sexual interactions to grade school students and throwing in fiction-based identity beliefs dampen the joy of childhood with adult themes. It is simpler to teach children that everyone is different, and all families are different, some more so than others. Teaching young students to not judge adult matters they are not old enough to understand is a much more effective solution. Subjecting very young minds to adult matters many adults can't understand or agree on is an afront to innocence.

The same liberals that keep books with traditional beliefs away from their children may insist on reading them trans and gender variant bedtime stories, or tales of how lucky they are having two dads. Progressives have the right to raise their own children according to their beliefs and lifestyle. They do not have the right to impose their beliefs on the minds of everyone else's children.

There are families that practice incest, does this justify teaching the intricate details of incest to all second graders? Should we enforce acceptance of incest as a normal condition. Children of incestuous families may have to feel left out in the classroom since the "I" in LGBTQIA already represents intersex. Adult matters are just that, for adults. Let the children be children without adult concerns.

Insurance companies have been sued for refusing to finance the intrusive, expensive, and excessive list of treatments the SOC deems medically necessary. Getting payment from any insurance company requires proof of liability and necessity. Elective procedures, treatments, and some therapies are not covered for the binary population. One example involved multiple trans women demanding insurance pay for feminizing facial reconstruction and voice treatments. These transwomen believed they were put in physical danger by having to appear in public with inadequate feminine facial features.

They claimed discrimination since insurance had paid for the facial reconstruction of victims of cancer deformities or traumatic injury. Notice the phrase reconstruction which in technical terms means return, repair, or restore to original condition. One of the transwomen that could afford the procedures claimed they no longer saw a laughingstock in the mirror after the surgeries and demanded compensation. Maybe they should sue WPATH for making their natural appearance a laughingstock in their own eyes.

The transwomen's lawyers suing the insurance company insist that WPATH and the Standards of Care (SOC) are supported by the medical consensus which the insurance company is willfully ignoring. The definition for the word consensus is general agreement. General agreement would encompass most of any given group, organization, or profession. As of January of 2023 there were 4,119 international members of WPATH, the originators of the SOC guidelines. By January of 2024 that number had dropped below 1,600, a loss of approximately 60%. This information is from a quick internet enquiry. Licensed physicians and mental health therapists number over 1 million in the United states.

Every doctor I broached the subject of gender theory with gave me an agitated look and responded that they did not want to discuss the matter. I imagine if I went to a gender clinic and asked the same question, they would be more than happy to discuss it. Gender theory is their mission in life and their bread and butter. Looking at the sudden drop in WPATH members in one year, it is obvious that their popularity has drastically faded on the world stage. The facts would seem to indicate that the SOC never had the medical consensus (majority) they claimed. WPATH is a paper tiger with an aggressive group of lawyers and well-placed connections in the medical decision-making process. They viciously attack anyone that questions their methods, claims, and beliefs. And they are ready to sic their rabid gang of followers on anyone that disagrees with them, from doctors and politicians to children that detransition.

Maybe it is time that doctors rose up and put an end to this mayhem and took back control of their medical boards. WPATH has a place in the medical field that can serve intersex people and the exceedingly rare cases of madness when someone actually believes they are trapped in the wrong body. They will have to at least try to ease their patients' suffering by helping them cope with reality and alleviate their stress rather than sell them false hope, fantasy and snake oil. Encouraging confused and atypical minds to hurt themselves medically and chemically to join a social club is not in any patient's best interest. Focus on healing the mind rather than pacifying it by damaging the body. Nothing is more noble than helping someone come to love themselves without hiding behind masks or disguises.

Accept the fact that transsexualism is a symptom of an emotional or mental illness, at the very least a personality dissociative disorder. No one can treat an illness without recognizing it is an illness first. Dysphoria is anxiety and nothing else, anxiety is real, gender science is not. Gender theory is self-descriptive; it is theory and an unproven one at that. Some claim the happiness transition brings is evidence-based proof. You can see the same happiness in the eyes of any alcoholic you give a bottle to. Both examples address what someone wants, but not their basic needs.

Now for a popular topic, drag queens. Drag was the expression used by men playing the parts of women in Shakespearean plays in the 17th century. Women were not allowed on stage in English theatres, so men would assume the parts of women in full attire. Excessive costumes and makeup for stage were commonplace, and the word drag is rumored to have come from their women's costumes dragging across the stage floor. This tradition stayed on as an artform which flourished again in the early 20th century.

Drag performers were popular along with burlesque shows at underground clubs and speakeasys during prohibition and some silent movies. At one point a drag performer was the highest paid actor in the United States. A drag performer could be straight, gay, or bisexual. Cross dressers were attracted to the idea of displaying their fetish in front of an audience, but many were in it for artistic value or the money.

Keeping with tradition, the garish costumes, make-up and overemphasized body language became a trademark. Drag was a popular entertainment adopted by the gay community in the early 30's with a continuous following that has evolved from underground gay clubs to cable television shows. A drag show is a performance, with the performer dressed and acting as the opposite sex, men as women and women as men. Until recently this was an adult only form of entertainment, usually paired with sex shows and strippers. With the current gender movement, a small part of the population feel it should be on full public display to all age groups. Acting jobs are hard to come by and drag performers jump on any opportunity to land a gig. Expanding their audience to include children and the public is in their best financial interest. It is an art form, but so is pornography if viewed through a purely artistic eye. The over emphasized body language and extravagant costumes can easily be viewed by the adult mind as entertainment or fantasy play. To a younger mind this display could cause confusion, blurring the lines between a character and a real person.

Canada's education department produced a film showing children placed in a room with a drag queen. One pair of young girls had many questions and trustingly accepted everything they were told by an authoritative figure. The two girls exhibited an open innocence and vulnerability to suggestion. In another scene with a teen boy, you could see his fear response to a potential predator. A grown man in drag placed in a room with a young teen boy, coaxing him into saying things he was obviously uncomfortable with, is disturbing. No normal parent can watch this without a protective response to end the predator's conditioning of their victim. Canada proudly lauded this film as proof that drag queens are harmless to children. Most viewed it as total dismantling of "stranger danger" only worse. It is telling children to ignore their sense of self-preservation at the cost of their own safety. Claiming that they are purely performers devoid of fetishism would be a logical point to make. The drag queens in the CBC film persisted in representing drag as who they are and not an act. What exactly is gained by a child's exposure to the sexually provocative display of drag and cross dressing? Very young children cannot differentiate between act, reality and fantasy.

One documentary was produced about kids in drag. Boys as young as 9 years old perform as little girls with sexually explicit dances and poses for rooms full of adults. The parents coach them to be as provocative as possible explaining that drag is as extreme "as the Sistine Chapel". The children's stage names are just as extreme; Lady Ga Ga and Queen Lactacia. Both the children and parents state that adults on the street are mean and cruel, not accepting their artistic interpretation, but they feel safe once inside the staging area. Somehow an audience peppered with pedophiles playing out their fantasies are deemed a worthy risk for the sake of art and a paycheck.

The progressive movement views these children as pioneers in the gender revolution, reveling in their commitment and freedom of expression. Many members of the progressive lifestyle are not comfortable with this exploitation of children but remain silent fearing retribution or excommunication from the alphabet community. It's all or nothing with these people and defectors are fiercely delt with.

The term alphabet gang is not sarcasm, it's easier to state than listing so many initials in an ever-expanding list of "inclusive" groups. Starting with the LGB which is sexual preference, adding trans and gender variant (queer), intersex which is physical, incels and asexual (not sexual) pan, 2 spirit etc., and the list goes on. In fact, inclusion has come to mean everyone except the straight, traditional, gender aligned majority that occupy the world. It's quite humorous to watch the Alphs speak at pride parades and functions pausing multiple times to list a half dozen initials and throw in a few plus, pluses on the end trying to include everyone. Any attempt to properly include the twenty or so pronouns render any monologue unintelligible. You would think Alph representatives would be self-aware enough to notice their message is lost in their long list of credits. No one sits through the credits at the end of a movie accept someone listed in the credits looking for recognition.

Gang or cult mentality requires the loss of individualism for the good of the group. Repetition of group identity and rhetoric, along with key words and chants suppress independent thought converting each member into a servant of the whole. The only difference between a servant and a slave is that one has willfully subjected themselves to servitude. With modern algorithms, news feeds and polarization, the question is not do I serve, as much as who I serve. Individualism is not conducive in a cult mentality because self-expression threatens the group's control, uniformity, and absolute authority.

Another topic that comes up from time to time is the treatment of trans inmates in prison. According to progressive thinking, anyone that makes the statement that they are trans must be taken at their word. This proves problematic in an institutional setting where basic resources are very scarce and rationed. Everything from living space, food, medicine and medical services are based on what is allowed per each inmate. This commonly means one doctor, one dentist, and one psychologist for up to 1000 inmates. Priority takes precedence over routine complaints, and yearly physicals are mostly nonexistent. For one inmate to require constant treatment results in less resources for another.

With limited employees, any irregularities in routine or distribution of resources causes strain on the system. Some prisons are much easier to manage than others depending on the security level and the type of inmates that populate them. Throw in an inmate claiming they are trans and suddenly the system becomes secondary to an individual demanding privilege. What's good enough for the general population is sub-par for the trans inmate.

Special housing and security, medications, surgeries, and pronoun use demands, drain and strain a system already in dire straits. This doesn't only apply to someone that's already Trans but to anyone uttering the word. It's not unknown for an inmate convicted for sex crimes with no Trans history to claim transition and demand confinement in a women's institution. It does not matter to the progressive movement if there is no Trans history. Everyone should have the right to transition at any time, without any question as to their motives.

For anyone not aware of prison mentality, every inmate will say or do just about anything to gain any advantage or privilege. Better housing, special diet, better treatment, anything of value is targeted by every inmate. Since prisons are segregated by sex, the chance to be with women tops the list. To don a dress and makeup to be with women is conceivably a legitimate hustle to many inmates.

Prison is not another place you go to when you misbehave, nor is it a place where your personal concerns are respected. The simplest freedoms such as showering, job selection and turning the lights on and off are no longer up to the individual. You are confined and totally at the mercy of your keepers for food, water, and housing. The priorities of any prison are in order; containment, prison property, prison employees, and least important the inmates themselves.

The guards learn quickly not to trust inmates or let their captives gain any advantage they can use as leverage. Inmates with important or sensitive jobs are given some privileges such as special housing or the guards look the other way when they notice contraband or gambling. When an inmate comes from a wealthy or privileged family the rules are bent the same way.

Each state has it's worst and easiest prisons. Inmates are assigned according to their crime, custody requirements, age, sex, health issues and availability of open bunks. Some states cater to Trans inmates giving them every possible item or service to assist in their transition, ignoring the cost to the other inmates.

In Florida the governor signed SB254 into law which prohibits state funds from financing gender affirming care, including prison facilities. This affected the 20 or so trans inmates housed in Florida's male prisons. The Alphs were enraged and demanded Trans inmates should be allowed to transition as women with the state footing the bill including surgeries. At the time of this writing, the case is still tied up in the courts.

Florida prisons have a Strict male grooming code that enforces only short or medium hair length not touching the collar or tip of the ear. The trans inmates complain that they should be addressed by their self-assigned pronouns and exempt from hair length restrictions for medically necessary reasons as described in the SOC. In a place where everyone is deprived of their most basic freedoms Trans still demand privilege. You would think that anyone in prison would have more to worry about, but then all inmates strive to obtain whatever advantage they can get.

In Theory and Practice

Change the narrative and change the mindset of any society's belief. There are progressive instruction manuals that give specific techniques to achieve this exact goal. Imagine watching a documentary that is narrated. The way the story is told by the narrator influences the way you process and view the facts. That is how you control the narrative. Changing the meaning of certain words and/or altering the description of a subject advances the agenda of the narrator.

Regarding transexuals, a group of medical professionals collaborated to delist transsexualism as a mental illness. Their main argument was that it is a natural condition with no cure or need to correct. If this logic were applied faithfully, every mental illness that presented as incurable should also be delisted. This is the one fatal flaw in their reasoning. In comparison a small number of Alphs assert that child molesters are born that way and should have the freedom to indulge themselves with absolute immunity. Another example is Therians.

A Therian is born with an innate attachment to one or more animals they identify as. Therians that identify as a wolf, will feel compelled to run on all fours and howl at the moon. They suffer from dysphoria because they are trapped in a human body. This is a real condition experienced by some people, many of which have families and are fully functional in society. They describe the extreme anxiety experienced from waking up every day as a human and internally referring to their human children as cubs. Therians are not to be confused with Furies which are more humanistic like a mascot at a sporting event.

Therians claim their identity is innate but how is that possible since they must first see an animal to identify with it? There are no differences in the descriptions of the thoughts and feelings of a Therian and the gender incongruent. They both feel disassociated with their body and imagine or fantasize becoming what they identify with. You would think the Therians would be welcomed by the Alphs but there is no gender or sexual element in their beliefs, though some Therians also experience gender incongruence.

By `blurring the definitions of male and female, then disassociating natural gender roles from birth sex, progressives have effectively changed the narrative. The gender movement sees itself as a necessary social revolution that will usher in the next stage of human social evolution where individual fantasies replace reality. The marginalized will rise up and vanquish 12,000 years of Human nature and all wars will end as people across the world join hands and turn vegan. The one thing missing in this equation are resources, there is only so much to go around. One resource is power, or who gets to run things.

In the Alph community there is more discontent and confusion than they like to admit. The trans and gender group look at the LGB as not being their authentic selves. The LGB just want to enjoy their freedom to love or mate with who they want without judgment. Other acronyms are constantly vying for more attention, crying marginalization by the Alphs. Which pronoun to use changes daily per individual along with what labels they place on themselves and each other. What insults one member brings gushing euphoria to another. In the process of destabilizing the English language to control the narrative there is only chaos within the gender theorists in terms of communication.

Hatred and cancel culture are slung at anyone not fully supporting the Alphs message of the day. It is physically impossible to keep up with the latest nuances in their beliefs. Alphs are a prime example of revolution for the sake of revolution. Give them everything they want, and they'll find a new cause to rally behind. Their time in the sun is beginning to decline as more countries distance themselves from the SOC standards. The majority of Americans have little to no tolerance of any gender agenda. The movement is shrinking but they won't go quietly, dragging the ACLU and other organizations into their legal fight for relevance and recognition.

The federal trade commission held a hearing addressing the "The Dangers of 'Gender-Affirming Care' for Minors." During this workshop physicians, whistle blowers, detransitioners and their parents testified about their personal and professional experiences with gender ideology. The FTC is investigating whether consumers have been exposed to false or unsupported claims about "gender-affirming care", especially as it relates to minors, and to gauge the harms consumers may be experiencing. That testimony indicated that practitioners of "gender-affirming care" may be actively deceiving consumers. The FTC is evaluating whether consumers (in particular, minors) have been harmed and whether medical professionals or others may have violated Sections 5 and 12 of the FTC Act by failing to disclose material risks associated with "gender-affirming care" or making false or unsubstantiated claims about the benefits or effectiveness of "gender-affirming care."

The FTC is not a court of law or a forum for debate. It is an agency created to protect the consumer from unfair or deceitful practices. The FTC has a long history of bringing enforcement actions concerning questionable healthcare and is uniquely positioned to investigate this potentially unlawful activity. Notice that the inquiry is focused on minors more than adults. Parents of detransitioners also testified how they were misled by gender specialists. If an adult can be deceived, what chance does a child have?

In most of Canada responsible minors can go to a healthcare facility and seek gender affirming care without parental consent. Similar laws were proposed in some states here in the U.S. where some adoptions were denied because adoptive parents would not support gender ideology. Some custody disputes were decided on the same basis. It is evident that a non-ideology-based family would not be a good fit for a trans orphan. In the same sense a religious or gender aligned orphan would be uncomfortable in an Alph household. To exclude one family for their beliefs and not the other is prejudicial.

Why not match the child with a family environment which best suits them? It doesn't require a whole lot of effort to make everybody happy. True to the gender movement's beliefs, only they and their kind should have the right to adopt. It's hard to imagine a progressive family taking a religious adopted child to church and socials. The more realistic scenario is a family outing to a Pride parade. This would seriously limit the number of adoptions if implemented nationally, since the Alphs are the minority and rarely physically reproduce by purely natural means.

An adult can make any decision they like to live as or believe in anything they wish. Whatever your sexual preference or gender ideology you are free to experience anything you wish. This is limited to not breaking any laws, or forcing others to do things against their will, physically or by intimidation. As odd or different as you may choose to be there is someone out there that's more than happy to indulge your desires and beliefs. No one needs to impose their will on others in disagreement. This is where majority rules. Most of the population do not need or wish to know all about you, your sexual habits or gender beliefs.

The majority of people follow the rules and social expectations everyone needs to follow that live in a society. Except for the handicapped, no one should be exempt from conforming to these rules. Since gender incongruity is a human condition, not an illness or a handicap, there is no reason they should require special considerations. It's easy for men to stay out of women's bathrooms, locker rooms and sporting events. Don't go where you don't belong. Belligerence doesn't make you intitled or an exception.

The progressives have all kinds of arguments about why their group should have exclusive rights that negate the rights of others. One argument is that sex is fluid, evidenced by the variations found in sexual birth defects. Alphs claim this is scientific proof that sex is not binary antiquating the separation of male and female spaces. In other words, men and women cannot be defined or positively identified because birth defects exist. Conveniently, the words defect, and abnormality have been purged from the progressive vocabulary as hateful and promoting stigma.

The progressive movement has now decided for everyone that sex is not binary but fluid, and gender can have any interpretation the individual chooses. They go on to claim that since women's bathrooms and locker rooms have stalls separating showers and commodes, no one can ever expose their genitalia to another person in a women's area. Let's include the clincher, that trans women are women and they belong with natural born women. These are all statements from men and women that pride themselves on their intelligence, education, and progressive views. They also laud the SOC as their bible.

Simply google "progressive narrative guidebook" and see how many sources have been developed and implemented by these educated elitists. These guides are a map of their intentions and motives to change society through controlling the narrative. Anyone not onboard is referred to as slope browed neanderthals displaying toxic masculinity. In the same breath they believe that on a sinking ship that men's lives are as valuable as women and children. Any other conclusion would be unfair; they also refer to the separation of men and women as sexist. Every word related to reality has been distorted, sex, gender, biology, even science has been opened to interpretation.

Any social revolution relies on the influence of children, which is much easier with social media. No child with a smart phone can escape exposure to their influence. The movement has managed to infiltrate the school system with gender themed books and lessons promoting how perfectly natural it is to not accept parts of your body or traditional gender roles.

The strange people are tired of being labeled strange. Rather than adapt, conform, or keep a low profile, they've decided to label themselves normal and everyone in disagreement a hater, enemy, or a phobe. Although they deny it, they are and have been coming for the children.

Some states have outlawed conversion therapy, a term used to describe an aggressive psychological treatment to return a patient to normality. Normality pertaining to a child's acceptance of their body and birth sex. Some conversion therapy may also include alignment of traditional gender roles with their birth sex or sexual orientation. By grouping all corrective methods such as reparative therapy under one label, the Alphs have eliminated any gender treatment other than affirmation therapy. Appling any corrective therapies are cruel treatment methods according to the SOC and progressive thought. By their standards you should never question any child's gender expression directly or indirectly. By the same logic you should never question any odd, erratic or questionable thoughts a child has that may cause physical or emotional harm.

If a child expresses the belief they can fly, breath underwater, or walk through fire you correct them and explain the human body cannot do that. If a child believes or insists, they are not the sex they were born as, the same explanation should take place. The progressive philosophy denies this most basic guidance a child requires to lead an informed and fulfilling life. They believe that sexual incongruence is not an issue that needs to be addressed or corrected in any child, toddler age through teen years. This is the SOC's definition of innate, accepting the self-diagnosis of a three-year-old that sips make-believe tea with their stuffed animals. What we can learn from children is the joy of innocence and imagination, not definitive social lessons that rewrite the history of human nature.

Place 20 of these same imaginative children on an island with no adults for ten years and watch how quickly the traditional gender roles will establish themselves. Human instinct and the drive to survive are our true innate traits. The strong will get the most and the best of resources while the weak will get the least. Rulers, workers and servants will emerge, along with conflict and negotiation. When you're worried about your survival and next meal, little time is spent on fantasy. Testosterone drives aggression while estrogen promotes tolerance and emotion. A Tomboy would be higher up in the pecking order than a feminine boy when strength and ability are valued necessities. In reflection, progressives are defying the very essence of human nature to neuter a child's instincts through informational neglect. Rather than letting children develop naturally with productive guidance, progressives suppress the nurture of nature itself.

One of the prominent progressive theories currently being promoted as gender studies fact is brain activity. Rather than claim the spiritual soul of an individual has a gender now it's a neurological misalignment of body and brain sex. There are some fantastic claims by progressive scientists that somewhere in the fetal stage of development something goes awry. This new theory claims that biology aligns the human brain to match the sex determined by the genetic code established at conception. In other words, nature develops the brain to match the XX or XY chromosomes in our genetic makeup. Since nature makes mistakes, now you can have a male or female brain that does not match your birth sex. They also claim some neural pruning irregularities also contribute to the mismatch of brain sex and body sex. It is plain to see that these new theories are manufactured and manipulated to support the "born that way" (innate) belief.

These scientific revelations check all the boxes for every progressive belief. The concept of a soul or a soul having a gender has been eliminated, pleasing many atheist gender theorists. The religious battle has been a stalemate with the futile argument God made trans what they are, and the need to transition is beyond their control. They have decided to fight the biological man or woman argument with their own biological explanation.

Progressives now concede that biological sex is male and female, but the brain may not match the body it is in. Now every brain has a gender orientation that is supposed to match the body it is in. Since nature is fickle, Trans and nonbinary brains do not connect with the bodies they are in. The brain will go on with its own sexual orientation regardless of what sex the body may biologically present itself as. In other words, now it is a brain trapped in the wrong body rather than a women trapped in a man's body, or visa versa. This is the exact same story with a different narrative. The convenient part of this theory is that nothing needs to change in the SOC or gender theorist's beliefs. Now they can claim scientific proof that they were right all along, and here's the PHDs in the lab coats to prove it.

There are notable differences in men's and women's brains. According to this new progressive theory, Trans and non-binary brains should now be detectable. This information can identify or disqualify whether someone is Trans or gender diverse for biological reasons. Maybe these new theories could indicate some predisposition, but they do not prove trans are "born that way" or innate. And what explanation is there for someone with a normal brain that does not align with their body? Neural pruning covers that situation, since it is impossible to map out that illusive brain activity that makes people trans or nonbinary at birth.

Another question would be, what effect do puberty blockers and cross hormone treatment have on brain development in children? Testosterone and estrogen directly influence brain development and puberty blockers stop that development altogether. The logical conclusion is that cross hormone treatment and blockers induce their results by chemically altering the brain and its natural development. Brain development cannot be undone and is not fully reversable as claimed. Only a fully mature brain free from alternate hormones could return to normal after exposure to cross hormone therapy. The human brain fully matures around age 25. Any hormonal intervention before this age would cause irreversible atypical brain development.

It would make sense to treat the brain to align with the body, this would alleviate the distress caused by gender or body incongruence. If you can alter brain development to match an identity, why can't you use the same techniques to align the brain with the body? Brain and body alignment is what nature intended according to this new gender and trans theory. This indicates that body incongruence is caused by a malfunction of this process.

A reasonable physician would attempt to assist the mind in realignment. Reinforcing and affirming a neural malfunction with cross hormones which alter brain development in children is not reparative, it is counterproductive. What cross hormone therapy and blockers do to the body are also destructive. This is another glaring contradiction in gender theory, it caters to a philosophy with a predetermined result, not a remedy. There is no cause to seek a remedy for an incurable condition now reclassified as a normal state of mind. The Alphs are assertive that trans behavior is completely normal. It is society that is wrong for not recognizing this. If only they could change the narrative!

Dr John Money was the first to coin the term "gender role" and was a major contributor to current gender studies. While working out of John Hopkins Hospital he specialized in infants born with ambiguous sex organs, hormonal cross therapy, and sex change operations. The last of which was discontinued by the hospital in 1979. He theorized that gender is much more than being male or female, establishing the notion of gender roles and gender identity. In 1967 he had the opportunity to use twin boys for a social experiment. One of the boys had been the victim of a botched circumcision. His recommendation was to raise the damaged boy as a girl with constant monitoring and affirmation therapy using the other twin as a control group. Dr. Money claimed to have proven that gender was something that could be learned and was not inherited with birth sex. This claim fell apart when the children grew older and the twin raised as a female insisted on acting as a male. This was despite female hormone treatment and constant reinforcement to be a female.

When the altered boy grew older, he publicly claimed he and his brother had been molested by Money along with other stories of unorthodox treatment. This boy ended up committing suicide in 2004. Although many of Money's theories have been disproved and condemned by the majority of health care professionals, he is praised to this day by progressives. He is a founding father of current gender terminology and theory.

This story is claimed as proof by modern gender theorists that male and female identity is established in the brain before birth and cannot be altered. Their oversimplified conclusion is that the brain is either male or female regardless of what body contains it. This is circular logic. Look at the story and what do you see? A male born male but raised female with cross hormones, surgery and affirming therapy is still a male just like the control group. Gender theorists ignore the experiment's findings. They insist that "if" the brain is female in a male body then nothing can be done to change that identity. That "if" is conjecture, since it is theory based and not scientifically proven or studied by Money's experiment. In fact, the opposite result had been revealed. The brain is not a foreign entity detached from the body, you are born male or female as a whole person. Biological sex is determined in the womb. Personal Identity develops after birth when an infant either embraces or denies how others identify them, this includes your name, sexual identity and descriptive biologically based pronouns. Trans activists still argue that their identity and fate are decided in the womb. I've pasted below a random argument one such gender activist posted online.

" Whether a person is a man or a woman isn't a matter of chromosomes or genitals, it's a matter of who you are. All the surgery and hormones in the world won't change who you are. No one can take that away from you, no one can force you to be anything other than yourself. For trans people,

hormones and surgery aren't about "changing a man into a woman" ... it's about helping a woman to be herself (and to help a man to be himself.)

You can inflict substantial damage on a person by forcing them to be something that they fundamentally aren't. Lots of trans people know what that damage feels like because an accident of birth and an ignorant and intolerant world force us to live a portion or all of our lives as something we fundamentally aren't. That damage claims lives every year. Just like surgery and medication help to heal the damage of a broken bone or infection, surgical care and hormone therapy can help to heal the damage inflicted by that accident of birth. Surgery and hormones can't turn men into women but it can help a whole bunch of us to be the men and women we really are."

This is the Alphs argument in a nutshell. Identity is the only reality. This identity determines what a man or woman is according to their interpretation. The physical body is only an accident to be delt with as an obstacle. Anyone that doesn't recognize this is ignorant, intolerant, and causing their (trans) deaths. How can you argue with someone like that. It's a little hard to accept a biological man telling women what a woman is. This is what is expected by the progressive movement and a portion of the medical community that encourages this behavior. Isn't it fortunate that transsexualism has been delisted as a mental illness? Any reasonable nonbiased mind would wonder how this type of thinking could be labeled normal.

We are not dealing with reasonable minds or theories. There is something known as social contagion. Put an innocent man in prison or a sane man in a mental institution for a few years and watch how their behavior mimics their environment. A normal person in a mob can be caught up in the moment. Now observe the digital environment everyone is exposed to. Dressing as the opposite sex is now therapeutic and no longer viewed as a fetish. A fetish by definition is focusing on an object (opposite sex clothing) or non-sexual body part that brings sexual satisfaction or euphoria. The simple act of trans changing their name is supposed to have just that effect. Why, because it indulges in fantasy, same as sexual role play.

It is not by chance that gender role is a term commonly used in the Alph vocabulary. If you indulge in a fetish you appease your dysphoria, the more you indulge the better you feel. Rather than admit crossdressing is fetishism, the euphoria it brings is credited to alignment with the true self. Another analysis would be that dysphoria is the extreme anxiety caused by denying the impulse to indulge in fetishism. Gender theorists would have us believe that fetishist desires are your true self that should be embraced, displayed and respected by everyone. It's simpler to claim cross dressing and trans identity is perfectly normal behavior while overlooking how few people agree with these beliefs. Remember that NAMBLA uses the same argument to justify the crimes of child molesters. All behavior is innate, you were born that way, it is a human condition that is unhealthy to deny. It's all in the narrative.

The Phoenix Complex

As long as humans have inhabited the earth there have been gender ambiguous people living amongst the masses. From Alexander the Great, powerful Romans, British royalty, and current celebrities, some people have wandered from the path of typical gender roles. Maybe the more influential and prosperous don't feel the need to hide their lifestyle, or their position of privilege lends to the occurrence of their behavior. We can't know everyone's mind or impressions and traumas from birth. But we can observe the behavior of others and gauge that against the bulk of society.

The higher the percentage of people that agree on any one subject, the greater the abnormality of those that disagree. Creating a baseline or definable normal state of any subject requires terminology everyone within a given population can agree upon. The ground rules must be set before approaching any thorough analysis of gender or trans theory.

The definition of a man or a woman has been scrutinized and described in the first chapter of this manual. It is a physical observable designation given to every human in terms of reproduction in nature. It is binary, one male and female are required to reproduce in nature. There are birth defects, these are defects in reproductive organs, genetics and genitalia, they are not other designated sexes. You are a man (male) or a woman (female) as defined for reproductive purpose. Intersex people can choose the option of which ever sex they most resemble or can perform as. They may remain ambiguous as an exception, but they are not the rule. Sex by natural design is binary. Sex and gender have become different subjects. Sex is physically observable while gender is a social construct based on common behavioral patterns attributed to each sex. Since sex is binary the common behaviors are binary along parallel lines.

Males are typically masculine, and females are typically feminine. The Y chromosome in males creates higher testosterone levels resulting in more aggressive, competitive, and logical traits. The estrogen in females lead to emotional, refined, articulate and nurturing characteristics. These different behaviors are also reflected in clothing, grooming, vocalization, and body language. At different times in history clothing and grooming may shift from masculine to feminine or vice versa. In the late 18th century, the word dandy was first used to describe a male highly concerned with his appearance and grooming normally attributed to females.

Other identifiers can be attributed to gender such as the colors blue and pink for boys or girls respectively. This color to sex association is less than a century old. Odd how born that way trans could be so strongly attracted to gender aligned colors that are only recently fashionable. Currently some male celebrities identifying as masculine have started painting their nails initiating a trend among the younger gender aligned population. This behavior by a straight gender aligned male would have been found unacceptable by his peers 30 years ago.

We have established there is male and female as a binary sex baseline. Masculine and feminine is the relative behavioral baseline we call gender. Everyone is included in this analysis, intersex and nonbinary are not exempt. Excluding yourself because you don't like the binary ground rules is a personal choice to not be self-inclusive. As of February of 2025, 9.3% of the adult U.S. population identify as LGBTQ. 56.3% of Alphs identified as bisexual while the rest split the difference. 1.3% of the nation identify as trans. Gen Z's coming of age is the indicated cause of the increase in numbers of Alphs and trans according to the Gallup report. These numbers reflect adults in the U.S. that are voting age. Gen Z with their digital childhood and need for identity will only swell these numbers as they age. The LGB core of the Alph community that are not trans are perfectly happy with the body they were born with and are not the focus of this analysis. Trans, nonbinary, eunuchs, and gender theorists are the primary focus group.

There is no single cause for transsexualism. Recently gender theorists claim that the brain is either male or female because of fetal development. This theory insists the body is incidental and should be altered if in conflict with the brain's predetermined gender identity. This ignores the physical reality of birth sex and its natural design. It also ignores impressions and trauma in early childhood development. It is without question an unproven theory. Gender theorists point to studies that suggest some medications used to prevent miscarriages cause the brain to develop this way. Once again, suggestions are not a proven fact.

Remember the Therians, they were born in a human body that doesn't match their animal brain. They suffer from the same dysphoria. Does anyone find it odd that an infant is born with a wolfs brain before ever seeing a wolf? By the same token how can a brain at birth differentiate the concept of sex or gender that it is not yet aware of? Common sense and logic dictate that sexual orientation, along with body and brain congruity are established after birth.

Humans rarely recall much from their first two years of life when the Id is formed from emotions, impressions and attractions it cannot fully comprehend. The Id only knows emotion, recognition, and desire. The Ego has its hands full in its early stages as it applies meaning and structure to an impulsive and emotional mind. Without proper parental example and guidance an infant's errant thought of incongruent identity can form. This is a logical assumption, more sensible than the "born that way" theory. I cannot prove this analogy is a proven fact any more than anyone can scientifically prove it is false.

Trans people are suffering; the debate is exactly what they are suffering from. WPATH would have us believe it is a perfectly natural condition to not accept the reality of what sex you are born as. 98.7% of Americans don't have this normal condition. If we use percentages as a gauge, we can consider this an abnormal condition. The bulk of Americans also don't believe they are a bird, a fish, or a wolf. Most Americans fantasize about being someone or something else, but we accept reality and don't fixate on the fantasy to the point of dysphoria. If everyone else can do it why can't the gender disoriented?

We all wish there was a simple solution that would make our lives better, but becoming someone else is not a reasonable option. You can disguise yourself as someone else, but you will always be you beneath the disguise. After full transition trans complain they still experience dysphoria. The response to this is living in the wrong body for so long has caused permanent trauma they will never recover from. Let's rephrase that a little; you can never escape reality. Every life story has a beginning, a journey, and an end. The end is not always a good one.

The trans journey is fraught with pain, trials and some jubilation, but it always ends with acceptance that this is as good as it gets. If they had only accepted and celebrated what they started with, their painful journey could have been avoided altogether.

Let's look at this painful journey and what it entails. First off, you'll more than likely lose friends, some or all family support and possibly a career. You will become a crossdresser, change your name and most likely begin hormone therapy. These hormones will change your body and emotional responses you've had throughout your life. Parts of your body will begin to atrophy or die off. You will have to take steroidal hormones the rest of your life to maintain a trans identity. Steroids cause blood clots, sterility, low libido, liver damage and other medical issues long term.

Women to men are more passable than men to women when it comes to voice and appearance on hormone therapy. Some may seek surgery to take it to the next level, amputating what would have been perfectly functioning body parts if not for the steroids. A good surgeon can alter nerve bundles so you can experience some sort of sexual stimulation, but that's not always successful. No matter what surgical work you have done you will never experience the same orgasm as your preferred chosen sex. As much as you deny it you will always live in fear when alone in public. Fear of discovery or being judged. Even Alph allies will scrutinize how convincing you look after your transition.

After all of this, you will continue to feel something is off. Now you must accept that this is as good as it gets, the journey is over, make the best of it. Is it everything you dreamed it would be? Rarely do our realized goals match what we imagined. Has the dysphoria completely disappeared, or have trans learned to bury or accept it? Transition demands a lot of sacrifice. Those that have transitioned or plan to will make any excuse to justify their sacrifice. Born that way is one such excuse, overwhelming desire is another.

No one argues that every American adult has the inalienable right to seek happiness in any way they see fit. To pursue medical interventions may be one of those goals. As laid out in the previous paragraph, the trans journey is not a pleasant one. Medicinal or surgical assistance on this journey should first require a full psychiatric evaluation before any therapy described in the SOC is applied. Below the age of 18, it should be legally forbidden to prescribe puberty blockers to anyone not suffering from precocious puberty or any hormones that are not supplemental or biologically reparative. Surgeries on juveniles should only be corrective and not alter normal development.

Supporters of gender theory should not initially perform or assess psychiatric evaluations involving gender or sexual incongruence. Such evaluations should only be performed and assessed by impartial professionals. If a patient may benefit from SOC guidelines after impartial assessment, all tests and analysis should be made available to gender specialists. Juveniles should be thoroughly questioned about why they want to be someone or something else. This is not a taboo line of questioning, but a diagnostic tool that can help an individual learn to accept their body, thereby alleviating dysphoria through psychoanalysis and medications if needed.

The born that way theory is only a theory, not a proven fact. Children should be thoroughly advised of this. Puberty blockers delay brain and body development that cannot be retrieved or undone, prescribing them while a child makes up their mind is a medical farce to prevent secondary sexual characteristic development. Cross hormone treatment in juveniles alter brain development permanently and should only be prescribed to mentally responsible adults.

In all fairness, Let's look at counter arguments commonly used online and shared amongst gender theory believers. You will see how science is used to back the born that way argument.

Sex — and hence, someone's felt-sense of their gender, what neuroscience terms interoception — is a complex of genetic, neurological, anatomical, and endocrine factors set in motion at around the 5th week of gestation and unfolding through a number of developmental phases through the second trimester.

This involves over 70 genes and there are numerous places in this cascade where things can zig instead of zag, resulting in an equivocal biological sex or gender identity involving one or a multiple of anatomical, neurological, chromosomal, genetic, and endocrine-signaling elements.

In plain words, it is possible for your body, your brain, your gametes, your genetics, and your hormones to have different biological sexes.

Sex & gender in humans is a lot more complicated that we learned in middle-school general science class.

The single thing that determines the direction this cascade takes is the SRY gene, usually-but-not-always found near the tip of the Y chromosome. In the absence of a functioning SRY gene, all anatomical, neurological, and endocrine factors default to female.

However, the SRY gene can be defective. It can be blocked by other mutations or missing altogether. The person's tissue can be insensitive to androgens. The SRY gene can turn up on the X instead of the Y.

Or there can be XXY, XXXY, XYY chromosomes, or 46,XX in some cells and 46,XY in other cells, or 47,XXY.

There can be mutations in key genes, notably AR that cause an under-masculinization of the brain.

And someone having one or more of these zigs will be born "trans."

And they "transition", not to become someone they are not, but to stop pretending that they are someone they are not.

This is a random argument copied from the internet explaining Klinefelter syndrome and its variations. You would need to have a firm grasp of genetics to truly grasp the intricacies of this syndrome. This is the layman's description from the Mayo clinic:

Klinefelter syndrome is a common condition that results when a person assigned male at birth has an extra copy of the X sex chromosome instead of the typical XY. Klinefelter syndrome is a genetic condition that occurs before birth, but it often isn't diagnosed until adulthood.

Klinefelter syndrome may affect testicular growth. This results in smaller testicles, which can lead to making less of the hormone testosterone. The syndrome also may cause smaller muscle mass, less body and facial hair, and extra breast tissue. The effects of Klinefelter syndrome vary, and not everyone has the same symptoms.

Symptoms

Symptoms of Klinefelter syndrome vary widely. Many children with Klinefelter syndrome show few or only mild symptoms. Most often the condition isn't diagnosed until puberty or adulthood, or it may never be diagnosed. For others, the condition has a noticeable effect on growth or appearance. Klinefelter syndrome may affect development, physical appearance, sexual development and mental health.

That's a convincing argument using science to explain how someone can be born trans. And the following explanation from the Mayo clinic lends credibility to the existence of this syndrome. The Mayo clinic refers to this condition as common with many experiencing few or mild symptoms. It is much more common than the percentage of trans in the U.S., so how does it directly correlate to born that way theory? Klinefelter syndrome does not condemn its victims to gender or sexual incongruence, sexual preference or the likelihood of dysphoria. Lower testosterone may cause fewer masculine features such as facial hair and smaller genitalia, but it usually goes undiscovered into adulthood. If this and other genetic birth defects are the direct cause for transsexualism a DNA swab test of every trans could confirm they are born that way. Gender theorists could publish the results and use it as scientific proof. They don't do that because it is only conjecture and opinion, not a scientific fact. In their own analysis "something zigs" and causes a trans birth. This equates to an undefinable random element. The whole idea is smoke and mirrors to support an archaic claim that trans is an incurable innate condition from birth. Here is a more complete description of genetic sexual mutations.

XX=female, XY=male, XO=Turner (female), XXX = Triple X (female), XXXX = Tetrasomy X (female), XXXXX = Pentasomy X (female), XXY = Klinefelter (male), XXXY = male variant, XXXXY = male variant, XXYY = male variant, XYY = Jacobs (male), XYYY = rare male variant, XYYYY = rare male variant, 46XX male = male = male (SRY translocation), 46XY female = female (AIS/Swyer), mosaics (e.g. 45,X/46,XX 46,XY/47,XXY = mixed traits, Chimeras (XX/XY) = mixed traits.

These genetic mutations do not make anyone another species of human. Just as genetic or sexual birth defects do not change the binary sexes of male and female. Irregularities in nature happen, that's why everybody is different. Binary theory is best defined in terms of male or female, this is observable fact. Notice the terms male and female specific in the above list unless specified otherwise. Every genetic variation above are either XX, or multiples of X and Y. Since X and Y are the only variables, sex is binary. Turner syndrome is an X and an incomplete X. Combinations with mixed traits only contain X and Y, there is no Z. To simplify this we will use a very basic example.

The Greeks based the world on the four elements of earth, fire, water, and air. Mix water and earth and you get mud.

More water makes thinner mud, more earth with less water create thicker mud. The different ratios do not make a new element. Scientifically mud would be expressed as a mixture of two elements with each element maintaining their individual properties just mixed together in various ratios.

The same can be said for the X and Y chromosomes as sexual elements. More X's or Y's in an individual's genetic makeup do not create a new sex chromosome, these are just variations of the binary elements of X and Y. No matter how you detect or mix them There is only the binary sexual elements of X and Y. This is scientific fact that cannot be disputed. We have established that reproductive sexual identity is biologically binary with compromised conditions creating some exceptions. We can now delve into the concept of gender.

Traditionally gender identity was synonymous with sexual identification in terms of male or female. The male and female bodies are physically different and become more defined after puberty. Since humans tend to clothe themselves against the elements, out of modesty or for decoration, direct visual identification of genitalia is usually obstructed. Clothing for men traditionally left more freedom of the legs, for both movement and less chafing from activity. Whereas women's clothing tends to cover the lower extremities almost to the point of hinderance at times. Through the ages women's clothing themes varied from modesty to amplifying sexual attributes. Skirt length and cleavage exposure varies from the oldest forms of art to modern days. Women were further subject to style trends such as beauty marks and the corset to acquire the hourglass silhouette thought fashionable to this day. Currently some clothing is shared by both sexes (jeans, T-shirts, hoodies etc.), though cut and tailored differently to accommodate the biological differences in men's and women's bodies.

Gender encompasses hair (facial and body), jewelry, makeup, body language, voice, behavior, and many nuances attributed to each sex as male or female. Gender appearance and behavior aligned with males is labeled masculine, while gender behavior and appearance aligned with females is feminine. Males are rough and tumble, more likely to take risks, suffer injury, go to war, and more expendable than females. Whereas females are more emotional based and traditionally shielded from danger or risks to preserve the species by producing and rearing the children and supporting family unity. In some societies women fight alongside the men though are rarely placed on the front lines where survival is less likely. In WW2 many resistance fighters were women that proved to be fierce warriors with little regard for self-preservation.

Women have been labeled as the fairer sex, but by no means are they lesser than men. Women are much more complicated than men with the emotional value they place on every thought or interest. While men pursue goals through logic and aggression viewing emotion as an impediment. These are some of the reasons that traditional gender roles developed and have remained consistent to this day.

Gender is defined as either masculine or feminine, these are the two opposing points directly associated with the binary principle of male and female. These points of reference can't move or disappear unless every human becomes self-replicating and binary sex becomes irrelevant. Since humans are mammals and not amoebas that's not changing any time soon.

All humans are different, and in being so can exhibit behavior contradictory to their biological sex. Males can act feminine and female's masculine. This can be momentary or continuous behavior depending on the individual. Gender is not a hard rule, but two separate points divided by degrees. Gender is not fluid, only the individual's behavior is variable when placed between these two points. You can have Tomboys, sissies, average, or extremes.

This variance in degrees is what the progressives refer to as "Gender Identity". For thousands of years people were identified as a whole individual, male or female, masculine or feminine, according to how they act or how their actions are perceived. There was never a need for labels, badges, or any form of identity which demanded respect simply because you say so. Social, authoritative position or military identities are earned and respected titles. Self-imposed titles are just that, a personal view of self.

Embracing gender theory begins with recognizing the importance of people's self-imposed identity or label. This only works if others of like mind accept this identity as valid and in return recognize this value in each other. The progressives place priority on this because of their established narrative that encompasses 10% or more of the population. When a child identifies as a non-binary, trans, pan-sexual they/them, the whole community is expected to celebrate rather than see it as a cry for help. Each of those descriptions are potentially suicidal. Some identities and accompanying pronouns are much more intense, like a contest of who is the strangest. Once again, sex and gender are not fluid, only the individual's interpretation is.

In the progressive view of reality, gender can mean anything you want. Your self-defining identity is the only reality, your true self. Whatever body you are trapped in is an accident of nature. Your true self must be recognized and celebrated; it is an identity beyond your control. Your gender identity is caused by a complex genetic coding with more X's than a game of tic tac toe.

Who and what you have decided (fixated) to be is your real identity which requires a real name, not the dead one someone assigned you. If your testicles offend you cast them off and become a noble eunuch, all puberty is bad. Puberty blockers, hormones, and surgery are good when it helps your body align with your true self. Let's not forget how miserable you will be, maybe suicidal from dysphoria, but cross dressing will ease the pain until the cross hormones kick in. If you believe this is a normal path of thought, you are mistaken. Take your head out of the rabbit hole and deny this simplified scenario does not encompass gender identity beliefs and theory.

Most tomboys and effeminate boys are not inclined to be trans any more than anyone else unless pushed by social contagion or poor advice. If their peers insist that gender theory is real and constantly coerce atypical children for capitulation, a weaker mind may cave into the pressure. Children can be very assertive in assigning labels to affirm their own beliefs.

Of the half dozen tomboys I knew growing up, none hated their sexual identity, and most of them fully embraced their femininity during puberty. All of them enjoyed being female, they just liked boy things and activities. You can imagine the physical and psychological damage these same girls would endure under today's progressive influence.

It makes sense in a child's mind if they are an effeminate boy or a tomboyish girl that it would be much easier to fit in as the opposite sex. This is a lack of self-respect for who they are. Their personal identity is clear, they know what they like. That doesn't mean that their body is wrong, they're just different from the gender norm. This is where gender and sex are totally different subjects.

If a girl has higher testosterone levels or a boy has lower testosterone, it would be medically prudent to test and correct their hormone levels. This may be caused by genetic flaws or some glandular imbalances. Hormone replacement therapy (HRT) means restoring hormones to normal levels for the birth sex of the patient. This is different from Cross sex Hormone Treatment (CHT) which uses steroids to induce development opposite of birth sex. HRT is corrective, while CHT is destructive to the natural sexual development of the human body. If there is a natural imbalance that affects behavior, appearance, and pubertal development why would any doctor make the imbalance worse with cross-hormone therapy?

Puberty blockers applied to the non-precocious do not address any imbalance whatsoever and halt critical natural brain and sexual development. The brain is part of the body, and it develops and matures right along with the body. The Alphs commonly use the term HRT when referring to any type of hormone therapy, this is intentional since CHT is obviously contrary to hormone corrective medicine.

Not all trans youth have been treated with puberty blockers and hormones. It is hard to pin down accurate numbers. Closest I could find was 1 in 14 of insured U.S. trans adolescents have had medical intervention. Surgical procedures are rarer under age 18 but they do happen regardless of claims to the contrary. The 2022 U.S. transexual survey listed 29% of adult trans having undergone at least one gender affirming surgery. That leaves 70% of trans being fully intact while dressing and presenting as women. That does not include the number of crossdressers (transvestites) that do not identify as trans. The number of young trans self-medicating from internet sources confuse the number further.

There are societal expectations concerning gender. Gender norms do not need to be explained; they are evident in everyday life in every society. If you are gender non-conforming or attracted to the same sex it does not indicate that you are trans. Your true self is the body and brain you were born with. Nothing can change your identity, the person you are and were born as. There is no reason to change anything. You don't need blockers, steroids or surgery that would make you less like who your true self really is. Dysphoria is magnified by listening to people that want you to change into someone else. They are telling you what they think you should be. What makes you think that you are so worthless and broken that you need to become someone else? Go ahead and wear clothes you prefer and act like yourself.

Stop trying to be something you are not, imitating something you think is better. You can't be them, and they can't be you because you are one of a kind. Why give up what makes you special? You were born with a name that is your identity, you don't have to become someone else, you are already you. You will never escape dysphoria by running from it, your dissatisfaction is in your mind, not your body.

Dissociative identity disorder is a listed mental illness, historically referred to as multiple personality disorder. If an individual has an alternate personality different or separate from their original personality, they may be suffering from DID. Bipolar disorder episodes can be so intense between highs and lows these behaviors may be misinterpreted as DID. Obvious signs of diagnosable DID are more than one identity displayed in a single person.

These identities can be different from birth sex or at odds with actual age. Typical causes are trauma that creates an alternate identity to shield the original identity from harm. This second identity can take on the job of protector at times of distress or triggers similar to what caused its origin. The original personality can retreat or hide from situations it cannot deal with, while its protector takes over to absorb the brunt of the trauma. DSM-5 requires amnesia or blackouts where the patient does not recall periods of time around traumatic events or during everyday life.

Repeated serious traumas can create more than two personalities, with different people (identities) showing up to deal with different situations, all emanating from a single person. Facial expressions, vocalizations, body language and sometimes a different name can emerge during a DID episode. Sometimes the alternate personality can completely take over and the original identity retreats into a dormant state never to return. This can happen at any age.

If a child in their first two years of life discovers that they are not the sex they mistakenly thought or wish to be, it could trigger such a traumatic DID event. The original young personality not having fully developed could easily be displaced by an alternate identity. This new identity has decided it is the birth sex the original could never be. This new identity knows how it should act, and what it should like according to its concept of its self-imposed gender. Any reminder by personal observation of anatomical differences to its chosen identity would be viewed as a point of distress or a feeling of disconnect. This new permanent personality may insist on an alternate name more in line with its view of itself since it is a completely separate entity with its own identity. Memories of the original identity wouldn't exist, and few people recall anything before the age of 18 months.

As the brain develops, neural pruning refines different parts of the brain that are used the most. Repetitive thought patterns relative to the imitated sex would refine the areas of the brain most like those found in the chosen sex. In other words, a two-year-old male acting and thinking like a female would exhibit brain development and activity similar to the brain of a normal biological female. The longer this occurs, the stronger the brain's likeness is to the chosen gender during brain development. By the time puberty occurs, the rising hormone levels and ever-evolving body development would cause a conflict that would be terrifying.

This is a much more logical scenario than the born that way theory. Newborns have no concept of gender until it is observed and interpreted, how can an unobserved behavior be innate with how much gender behavior encompasses? Trans people claim they knew from as far back as they remember that they were born the wrong sex. That would be true if the alternate personality was created just for this purpose. Any questioning of this entity's reality would be interpreted as a threat to its very existence. By the time puberty starts this trans alter ego would be well imbedded and incurable by design.

I propose a possible treatment towards the end of this manual that has been very successful with therapy resistant PTSD.

Since PTSD may be the core source of trans dysphoria, there may well be a cure that actually treats the source of this anxiety. This treatment requires professionals that would dedicate their abilities to serving their patients' needs and well-being more than an ideology.

One of the more baffling recommendations of the SOC is encouraging trans patients to change their name. WPATH, and the trans community place so much importance on this one element. (SOC8 page s107 statement 11.5) Trans insist this process is essential to transitioning. In this process the birth name is detached from their identity, and termed dead, never to be used again. A new name is chosen and any references to their birth identity is considered irrelevant, an insult, and an assault on their well-being. The new name, clothing, pronouns, and mannerisms are a form of rebirth from the ashes of the life they were previously forced to endure. A descriptive label for this symbolic ritual would be the Phoenix Complex. This approach (affirmation therapy) functionally encourages the patient's disassociation from their physical body. The same body that already has a name and sexual identity.

This new name, gender, and everything this new identity chooses to incorporate is now the only true self. Affirming body dissonance and discouraging any doubt by either the juvenile trans patient or their parents. All of this occurs under a doctor's supervision, backed by an ill-conceived notion one physician used to achieve fame over 60 years ago.

The progressive view of gender is however the individual may interpret it. Gender theorists maintain that societal expectations of behavior assigned to sex at birth (gender) is invalid, archaic, and destructive. Society represents the bulk of the population and their interpretation of what is feminine and masculine. The progressives claim that only their definitions of gender have any valid meaning. The term gender nonconforming would be an ideal example of this, if not for the recognition of the binary nature of gender. You must have an established system in place to not conform to. The Alphs also claim sex and gender are not directly connected in their world, they tend to use either term at their convenience when erasing the lines between male/female and masculine/feminine.

Transexuals don't accept their birth sex, in the purist terms they identify with the body of the binary opposite sex. But it doesn't stop at the body, they want to conform to society's expectations of the opposite gender. You can play games with definitions and labels, but everyone really knows what a man and a woman are. Real men and woman do not need to define themselves or adhere to any expectations because they are authentic. Real men and women were born, identified, experienced childhood, puberty, and finally adulthood. Puberty was tough for everybody, your body changes while hormones awaken drives and feelings that are essential for physical and emotional growth. All natural men and women experienced doubts about their identities, image and their place in this world. This is what it means to be natural men and women. We are the sum of all our experiences, that's what makes us real.

Trans people will never experience what it takes to be their chosen sex and gender. They can only immerse themselves in the stereotype they've observed and identified with. Trans never masperienced the natural menstrual cycle or nocturnal emissions of the opposite sex or the psychological impact these had during puberty. The male to male or female to female bonding that takes place during childhood and throughout life are birth sex specific. Trans can only imitate observed behaviors, they have never experienced the journey behind them.

No one denies the existence of trans men and women. The difference is the prefix trans, which automatically excludes them from the category of simply men and women. Real people are truly authentic, Authentic definition; *not false or imitation: real, actual.* The great majority of people don't really care how you identify, what you do or how you act. The moment a minuscule segment of society dictates the identity, reality and validity of the majorities established norms, you've created a conflict.

Distorting definitions of sex and gender, making statements like "trans women are women" and legally forcing school children to learn your alternate ideology is not diversity, it's divisive and destructive. This is not an opinion but observable fact. The evidence is the high rate of suicidal tendencies exhibited by gender nonconforming, trans, pan-sexual, and alternate lifestyle children. This is the gift progressives envision as the future of the human race. Social revolution does not equate to human evolution. The drop in birth rate is one such indicator. Absence of the natural drive to procreate has been replaced by an identity choice.

Summary

Transexuals or trans have existed since time began and will continue to exist as long as humans walk the earth. Some people may not like this fact, but nothing will ever change that they are here to stay. With the rise of social media their presence has come to the forefront of debate reaching as high as the Supreme Court. What was once a discreet lifestyle has now become an overt movement as people have developed the need to wear their identity like a billboard for everyone to admire. The Trans Manual attempts to explain the facts and dispel much of the misinformation both sides present as indisputable fact.

There is no question that some people refuse to accept the sexual identity they were born with or the gender that corresponds to that sex. Terminology like "assigned at birth", "sex and gender are fluid" was created to invalidate traditional norms and definitions. The fact that a portion of the medical community promotes this alternate vocabulary proves just how deep a social movement has embedded itself into our most trusted institutions.

Psychological evaluations, therapy, hormone treatments, and a variety of surgical procedures have produced a cash cow with lifelong consumers. Not all physicians agree with gender theory, not anywhere near the majority. Dissenting physicians are ostracized and harshly ridiculed in public by the same medical boards created to protect all doctors and patients. A number of concerned doctors that endorse the Standards of Care have been questioning their young patients' ability to understand the long-term consequences of their choices. When the WPATH tapes were exposed on the internet, the general public witnessed the blatant disregard of some gender doctors' concerns by other WPATH supporters.

Gender theory supporters have come up with some truly great genetic and embryo developmental reasons for transsexualism. These are theories constructed to support the born that way ideology. They would have everyone believe our gender identity and sexual preferences are predetermined at birth and we have no free will or choice in the matter. Were this true, every personal decision and outcome is pre-scripted and every choice we make is an illusion. It would be very unlikely that this only happens to trans. Every human alive would be predetermined as gay straight, bi, gender aligned, or gender incongruent. Our favorite color preference would also be predetermined before our eyes and brain ever registered its existence.

During and after puberty hormones determine some behavior but not every thought. If someone whimsically decides to become bisexual, trans, or gay later in life it's doubtful that decision was determined prebirth. It is much easier to blame nature than analyze what thoughts and influences brought a trans individual to their current state of mind.

WPATH and their representatives on the medical boards claim transsexualism is not a mental disorder, it is a human condition that often causes dysphoria. Rather than address the condition that causes dysphoria, doctors alter the properly functioning body to match the atypical mind. The human body is an organic machine, if a machine malfunctions you repair the damaged part, you don't redesign the machine to match the faulty part. Transition mimics this principle by altering the human body's purpose. To alter a healthy properly function body equates to making it ill or partially nonfunctional.

A cross dresser can reverse their appearance at any time. Once cross hormones are applied certain glands and organs begin to deteriorate, at some point the damage is irreversible. If reproductive organs have been removed or damaged supplemental hormones become an involuntary life sentence. An adult has every right to choose this destiny, but a juvenile has no concept of lifelong implications. The human body is meant to grow and then mature through puberty into adulthood, emotionally as well as physically. Any disruption of this process is destructive and not physically or emotionally advantageous.

Puberty blockers for non-precocious children have no long-term studies. To claim they are safe with no side effects is an unproven assessment. Hormones used in replacement therapy have known side effects, used in cross gender treatment even more so. Cross hormone therapy can result in irreversible changes to the body within a few months. Long term use can result in deteriorating or atrophied gonads and vaginal walls, accompanied by a higher probability of stroke and cancer.

Any surgery carries the possibility of complications including but not limited to infections, loss of sensation, scarring, nerve damage, and loss of bodily function(s). Any or all of these conversion therapies are no guarantee that dysphoria will vanish or dissipate. Many trans feel great relief once any or all of these procedures are completed only to have new problems arise such as sexual libido, nipple and genital sensitivity, having to stretch artificial vaginas frequently, shallow vaginal depth, tearing at the surgical site, or a feeling of broken glass if an erection does occur. A person would be very desperate to put themselves through any such ordeal. That is why transition should be approached as a last resort, and not a casual remedy to be thrown at any three-year-old or adolescent experiencing an identity crisis.

It has become obvious that the medical community has failed to police itself. WPATH and the SOC were founded to treat the slimmest of minorities that had an incurable condition causing intolerable distress that drives them to self-harm. Physically damaging people for the sake of a form of vanity was never the original intent.

Cancer and AIDS were once viewed as incurable, but doctors and researchers never gave up trying to find reparative treatments. Patients with these afflictions were made as comfortable as possible, while science continued to search for cures and treatments. AIDS is well under control with medications while many cancer patients are living longer better lives. Never once did doctors claim these illnesses should be delisted as an illness and focus solely on treating the symptoms. That is what the medical community did and continues to do in the case of transgenderism.

For the WPATH Standard of Care to promote futility for a condition that is the cause for such human discomfort appears grossly negligent and unethical. You don't need to be a doctor to know when an arm is broken, you set it to heal and treat the pain. To prescribe pain killers and ignore the broken arm is ignoring the cause. Gender theorists refuse to address the cause; they refuse to admit there is a problem. Were gender incongruence not a problem with a cause, there would be no dysphoria. It is so convenient to blame society, genetics, and nature itself before focusing on the true source, the individual mind.

Recent research into Psilocybin therapy has made remarkable advances in the treatment of depression, PTSD, and anxiety. At this time there are few doctors that specialize in this technique which has reduced anxiety and depression in 65% of patients once deemed incurable. One study showed 4 out of 20 patients' depression went into remission. A single 8-hour session with a psilocybin therapist has proven more effective than decades of talk therapy alone with long term results. Continued talk therapy after treatment amplifies the results. This is an established treatment researched at John Hopkins since 2006. What a great treatment for dysphoria if only there were an illness to treat. Psilocybin could well be the cure for transsexualism for some, while at the very least alleviating dysphoria for others where the SOC has failed. Psilocybin in the hands of the SOC supporters would likely be used to affirm gender theory in an open vulnerable mind rather than seek out and treat the original trauma. WPATH would never allow their innate theory to be questioned. Remember, the SOC states that no cure is required for transsexualism, it is a normal human condition.

Social contagion is real, and it exists in multiple forms such as imitation, mirroring, and herd behavior. Social contagion can be induced by forced exposure such as online algorithms or disguised as empathy, another form of social contagion. Teaching gender theory to young children induces empathy, requiring the young mind to see alternative genders through the eyes of the incongruent. M&W definition of Indoctrinate; *"By the 19th century, indoctrinate was being used in the sense of teaching someone to fully accept only the ideas, opinions, and beliefs of a particular group"*.

Let's assume that gender theorists and the progressive movement in general qualify as a group. Teaching tolerance or awareness of other people's beliefs does not require complete personal acceptance and obedience to those beliefs. Nor does tolerance require a thorough dissection, analysis and memorization of gender theory and pronouns in a second-grade classroom. Tolerance is recognizing and accepting the fact that other people are different, it does not demand participation in those differences. There is a notable difference between tolerance and indoctrination.

Inclusion means acceptance not dominance. To be included is to participate in any group act as an equal while adhering to the same rules as everyone else in this group setting. The group sets the rules by majority rule as in team sports. Each team respects the common rules to promote fairness in competition. Age group rules prevent an 8-year-old from competing with a 15-year-old, female competition is commonly separated from male for the same reason. Males are physiologically different from females in too many ways to be ignored. Size, stride, muscle mass, lung capacity are different, even more so once puberty occurs. Unless it is agreed by the majority of participants in any sport that sex is a non-issue, male and female sports are segregated. Males competing against females is not fair, neither are trans males on steroids competing against other females. The rules are set to level the playing field by excluding anyone that falls outside the rules. It's a very simple concept that trans and their allies refuse to recognize. Insisting the rules don't apply to some individuals is an assertion of privilege. Privilege only exists at the expense of others. No one is keeping any biological male from competing in a dress, so go compete with other biological males dressed as a girl. If you do well and impress the team, no one will care much.

Steroid use is outlawed in most competitions. If you're a serious athlete stop taking steroids and then compete on a level playing field. No single person should have a fabricated unfair advantage in organized competition. This is known as cheating or a "Ringer" in the sports world. Ruining it for everyone else to make a social statement is not a team player mentality. There is no "I" in team.

Drag is an adult form of entertainment that should not take place in a public setting. Libraries and school rooms are not an appropriate setting where children can accidentally or intentionally be exposed to an adult theme. A sexualized adult that focuses on children should be a red flag to any parent. The progressive argument is that exposing children to drag is harmless and educational. In reality the intent is to normalize aberrant behavior. Clowns have a reputation for causing stress in many children with their painted faces, garish outfits and hair. Drag queens have no less effect and many similarities as both are entertainment focused. Drag has the added sexual element, whereas clowns are more humor aligned.

The core element of the LGB has been unhappy lately about their pride parades having been hijacked. Once used to celebrate the stonewall incident that resulted in the LGB rights movement, something has changed. Pride parades in recent years have become decadent displays of fetishes and sexuality with leather clad S&M participants walking their slaves on leashes and performing overt sexual acts in public. Drag queens and drag children sashaying in the streets along with sexualized Furries have driven some core LGB to quietly boycott these events.

Many LGB have children they don't want exposed to behavior they deem deviant. Just because some people are same sex attracted does not mean they are without morals or fail to shield their children from aberrant behavior. Publicly complaining about this mutation of the LGB message will be swiftly answered by this new radical progressive movement. They demand complete obedience, where normality is shunned and abnormality is celebrated.

Bathrooms and locker rooms are divided by sex, not gender. Some claim this is irrelevant since they had skinny dipped or undressed with family or friends without issues when young. That does not take into consideration the vulnerability most people feel in a state of undress around strangers or adversaries. Some privacy from the opposite sex when vulnerable is expected in public or school bath and locker rooms. This was never a problem before the gender crowd decided to demand privilege. Everyone knows what a male and a female are, you have a penis at birth, or you don't, size doesn't matter. Some trans after hormones and/or surgery are very hard to detect. Sometimes trans can appear more male or female than natural men and women. This has led to altercations when Bearded ladies with deep voices enter the appropriate restroom or masculine appearing natural women are misidentified.

The only solution to this problem is a new form of ID. Sex cannot be changed unless intersex develop opposite identification at birth. ID should have birth sex male and female designations, and separate gender male and female designators. This is the only quick answer to prevent altercations.

Some will claim that a male that has undergone complete female conversion has no interest in spying on women in locker rooms. This is a false statement since gender expression has no influence on sexual attraction, that is an assumption and not fact. Otherwise, trans men wouldn't get pregnant, and intact trans women wouldn't impregnate them, or gender aligned women.

Trans women after complete transition can perform as a lesbian, gaining access to women they could never attract as a man. This is not as unusual as it sounds. On the other end of the stick, there are trans men that wish to dominate natural men by artificial means, this is the ultimate proof of their adopted manhood. The two point system of ID (sex and gender) would end the question of who belongs where, while protecting natural people with ambiguous appearance.

The radical elements of any belief are easily offended. Everyone likes to take everything personally and feel the need to express their opinion in the most boisterous form. Thanks to social media and biased news reporting, any subject becomes a rallying cry. When celebrities voice an opinion as if offended all of their followers are expected to react in the most violated way. Politics and religion have been using this same principle for thousands of years. This is why the extensive religious opinion of sex and gender has been intentionally omitted from this manual. We are dealing with facts and science that can be verified through observation. Religious interpretations and references vary greatly along with which sources are used to base opinions.

Many conservatives may think this manual is supportive of the Alph community or at least the LGB portion of it. This publication is a neutral opinion to encourage the individual right to pursue happiness in whatever form it may take as long as it doesn't hurt someone else. When contentment illudes some people, they tend to encourage discontent and discomfort in others. This is not this manual's intent. The focus of this manual is gender theory, transsexualism, and the observable arguments and beliefs for and against this subject.

There is no doubt current progressives and gender theorists endorse changing and physically altering people. Adults should have the right to pursue what makes them happy without expectations of the world celebrating their decision. Children on the other hand will have to settle for dressing up and playing the part of the identity they choose, without chemical or surgical intervention. This is not cruel as many will complain. If as an adult they decide to transition, their correctly developed bodies will have enough flesh to perform bottom surgery. This will avoid removing flesh from other parts of their body, resulting in a better surgical outcome. Or they may outgrow the impulse to physically transition, without the constant pressure and expectations self-imposed by starting the transition process. In this situation their body will have matured correctly with normal appearance, sexual function and libido. It is a win-win situation with the best outcome for juvenile trans.

One final note to WPATH, as a science-based organization you should question every theory and conclusion with an unbiased view. Nearly 39 percent of Americans will be diagnosed with cancer throughout their lifetimes, yet we don't consider this an acceptable normal condition.

Currently 1% voluntarily identify as trans in the United States and WPATH considers this a normal condition, not an illness, or a problem to investigate addressing. If you cared about the symptom of dysphoria, you would use all those scientific minds to research the cause to treat the source of this specific form of anxiety. The cause is body disassociation which is a mental illness. Ignoring this fact disqualifies WPATH as a science-based methodology. Accepting the core belief that transsexualism is incurable without question confirms it as a faith-based organization.

Gender gospel is the SOC rewritten to appease WPATHs membership, currently saturated with trans activists. When rapid onset gender dysphoria was researched, WPATH discredited the results over a patient release issue and a peer review signature. WPATH refused to consider the theory's possibility as a tool to correctly diagnose the differences between trans and the easily influenced.

Any question of faith in the innate theory is instantly attacked just as this manual will be criticized. And why should gender misalignment require changing the body? Gender is a construct encompassing clothes, grooming, behavior and overall appearance. Sex and gender are completely different issues; one does not rely on the other in your own progressive belief system. Body disassociation would be a better terminology. If the mind begins life with a predetermined sexual identity and sexual preference, then everybody's favorite color is predetermined before their eyes and brain get to identify it. Think about your favorite color every time you use the word innate. Science and logic can be so eye opening when you apply it without preconceived bias.

Point and Counterpoint

For human procreation there are only two sexes in nature, male and female. The genetic anomalies some theorists claim are other sexes are mutated variations of the two sexes which still contain the binary of X and Y. X and Y reproductive chromosomes are the basis of all mammalian life without exception. Gender reflects the nature of these two sexes as much in behavior as in purpose. We are quasi slaves to our hormones combined with instinct and nurture. The two genders which reflect binary sex are masculine and feminine. This equates to the behavior and appearance most exhibited by males and females in societal settings. Since everyone experiences feelings or expressions attributed to either male or female there is no distinct line in the sand as to 100% gender congruence. It's more a generalization of expected behavior and appearance.

How someone identifies can fall into the normal expected pattern or in opposition of the norms. A biological male, no matter how he acts or appears will still be a male and the same for natural born women. Identifying as, or assuming the role of the opposite sex is pure mimicry of observed stereotypes since anything a male thinks, believes, or does, he is still a male. The same principle applies to women. Intersex is the exception and not the rule, they have the options of both or either sex, in that sense they are unique.

When it comes to women's spaces their privacy is a small but vital expectation of safety and domain for women only. Most natural men support and respect this accept predators, the poorly raised, and the belligerent. Trans women are men no matter what appearance or surgeries they have had. Once again men are targeting the last safe spaces women have. It isn't that hard to respect women's basic rights. Trans women are men that chose to appear as women, whether they think they were born in the wrong body, feel dysphoric, or simply find the trans identity appealing. Regardless of the reason, or doctor recommendation they made a conscious decision to imitate women in appearance.

Bathroom bills don't target trans gender individuals; they target men in women's spaces, and women in men's spaces. Progressives argue everybody has the need to relieve themselves, why should women require special protections. The better question is why should trans? If all areas of privacy were to become unisex, there would be no privacy, and trans women would be in the same room with the same men they say make them unsafe. So, women's safe places are only valid if certain men are included?

Progressives demand respect for trans identity while completely disrespecting and trampling one of the few rights natural women have. Respect is a two-way street and that is the conundrum that progressives and the trans community have created and continue to pursue. You will never gain respect until you return it. This is such a simple concept which seems to elude this educated and lofty group of progressive believers.

What does it mean when someone claims to be trans? That depends on who you ask and which way the wind is blowing that day. There was a time when different behavioral situations had specific labels that made identification simple. When someone cross-dressed for stimulation or sexual gratification they were called a transvestite, it is a fetish.

Medically changing yourself to appear as the opposite sex was termed a transsexual. Autogynephilia is when a man was aroused by the thought of his body having a vagina. Women wanting to become a male was casually labeled penis envy, though that too falls under the transexual label. Drag queens could be an erotic art form or embrace any of the previously mentioned traits.

All these gender presentation identities and more are now under one umbrella, the word Trans! And it is a magical word. Simply by saying you identify as trans means you instantly become one. You don't need any medications or surgeries. You don't even have to dress the part, saying the word means you are now a member of the trans community.

About 29% of adults that claim trans identity have had at least one gender affirming surgery. That means 70 percent of trans adults are fully sexually intact while claiming to be the opposite sex. In a 2022 study by the Williams institute 1.4 percent of children ages 13-17 identified as trans. Of those, 1 in 14 had actually sought treatment under private insurance. This does not include Medicaid or the uninsured. These numbers leave a lot to be desired in accuracy, but loosely we can estimate that 12 out of 14 or 6 out of 7 juvenile trans are self-diagnosed. Yet their decision to identify as such is fiercely defended by progressives, gender theorists, educators and some in the medical community.

Lack of parental guidance, peer pressure, mental or emotional disorders, and sexual confusion, can all contribute to a child misidentifying themselves. Yet under the trans umbrella they were all born that way. Gender theorists claim the internet, peer pressure, and mental disability have no influence on this gender transitional phenomenon. Forcing memorization and understanding of gender theory and identities in second grade classrooms cannot influence a young mind to question their gender, it can only enlighten them.

Enlightenment is a lofty word for indoctrination in this particular instance. And the people pushing this ideology consider themselves enlightened. They have imbraced an overwhelming need to spread their beliefs to prove that their view of the world is correct. They need it to be true or everything they believe is just a foolish lie.

The word transvestite has a stigma, so it should only be called cross dressing now. That makes sense since the SOC recommends cross dressing to children as affirming therapy. You can't medically prescribe a fetish now, can you? Don't ever use the words amputation or castration, it's now labeled compassionate gender affirming surgery. There is a distinct difference between a true correctly diagnosed transexual and the others that fall under the umbrella, though the gender activists will claim differently. If, an actual biological cause is ever discovered for transsexualism, it would likely exclude over 95 percent of the current trans population. The movement would then claim there are other causes not yet discovered. Or that it is a neural pruning issue independent of provable biology.

You shouldn't hate a person for being trans. They can be some of the kindest people you'll ever meet. But their appearance can be unsettling to the average person, making it difficult to ignore or look past. There is also the concept of guilt by association. When the average person sees someone trans, they mentally visualize a man in a dress following their daughter or wife into a woman's rest room. Or someone supporting online videos of little boys in dresses shaking their hips and posing erotically on a stage for cheering adults. Let's include men competing against women in sports. These are some symbolic triggers that many people associate with trans expressionism.

The aggressive "accept all or nothing" attitude of many progressives leaves the majority of people rejecting everything they stand for. The original LGB community had finally reached acceptance and credibility, which now fades because of gender association. The radical gender element rants and raves like a spoiled child practicing every kind of misbehavior seeking a reaction. Then they scream persecution when society does respond. Everyone sees these voices as representatives of the whole progressive movement.

A common grouping of their mantras is "we stand together as one" right after they say, "trans women are real women." Accepting everything or nothing with no tolerance for any dissension leaves little choice for those with common sense. Few people not swayed by herd mentality will accept the long list of progressive beliefs they demand you pledge fealty to. You can support most of their beliefs but disagree with one of them and be publicly labeled a bigot and a hater.

You hear many complaints about how unsafe it is to be transgender. "Hundreds are murdered every year just for being who they are". But they don't mention how many were killed by their own kind, boyfriends, or significant others. Others are killed selling their wares in the high-risk sex trade. Trans women are 49-66 times more likely to contract HIV. Trans men are estimated at 6.8 times as likely. This is not a healthy choice, nor a perilous path children should be encouraged to pursue. It's very common for children that are abused to grow up and become abusers themselves. There's a good chance that many trans want to share their trauma on a subconscious level while encouraging others to join them. No one wants to suffer alone, and solidarity is often a derivative of mutual suffering. The internal support aspect of the trans condition is the only admirable result of a movement that negatively affects their health while exposing them to peril.

In a laboratory, female mice had a gene blocked which resulted in them not defending their nest or young. But they did not mimic male mice. There is absolutely no confirmable scientific proof of what causes the trans manifestation as an innate condition. Common sense dictates it is developmental, adoptive, or appealing to some individuals. Quoting decreased suicide rates with gender affirming treatments confirms a decrease in self-harm when people are given hope that they can physically change their sex. Affirming therapy is not the direct cause of lower numbers, it's the promise of the hope it brings.

People hear what they want to hear when it comes to hope. They see themselves becoming what they wish to be. Affirming therapy offers a path to obtain a goal that in reality is unobtainable. Yet in the mind's eye, it's everything the gender conflicted could wish for. They get the opportunity to change their sex and the promise that others will accept their identity. Exact data is unclear, but the greater majority, 75-90%, do not get the full surgical conversion. Many trans identifying have also been altered through medications. Yet they all identify as the opposite sex as they are medically instructed or inclined to do as part of their identity. The main point trans focus on is that they are perfectly normal. The meaning of Normal: *is conforming to a type, standard, or regular pattern : characterized by that which is considered usual, typical, or routine.* merriam-webster.com 2025. Shall we change the definition of normal next or is that ambiguous also?

If you want to embrace your oddness, what makes you different, then revel in your abnormality. But do not claim you are the standard of the human race that every human evolves around. Your sphere of influence stops with your own kind which you make quite clear with your labels. How can 1.4 percent of the population cause so much turmoil? Trans account for less than 20% of the Alphs. They've tried to recruit black sympathy and pro-choice advocates in their pursuit of controlling the narrative by increasing their numbers. If it was harmless to children like hippies having long hair or goth painting their nails black, no one would care much. Chemical alterations and indoctrination into an alternate reality where you can pick your sexual identity from a list is a bridge too far.

In the Gender world The SOC is their bible, and everyone else is labeled Cis, this is not coincidence. This is a new religion, one that was first conceived as a medical treatment in 1966 exclusively for transexuals and now supported by the trans umbrella. You will have to accept and testify to the world that you are trans, and in return they give you liberating hope. The faithful will be rewarded with community and love, leave the movement and expect ostracization and abandonment. The biggest problem with any belief system is the fanatics it attracts.

Progressives claim that they ask for very little, just the same basic rights as everyone else. This includes subjecting children to sexual information in grade school through sensual literature or required gender lessons. Refuse to date a transgender and you are a bigot. Progressive activists refuse to recognize that women have any right to privacy from men. They do insist that men identifying as women are entitled to that very thing. They alone have the privilege of intruding on the opposite sexes' privacy. Equal rights mean you follow the same rules as everyone else. How can you demand rights you deny everyone else and call it equality?

The current minimal definitions of gender that progressives agree on are separated into four parts. Gender assigned at birth, male or female name along with expectations of future sex aligned expression. Gender identity, the personal sense of being masculine or feminine regardless of birth sex. Gender role, the expected behavior of birth sex as displayed by the bulk of society. And gender expression, which is the outward appearance and behavior of feminine or masculine stereotypes as expressed by the individual. Though gender theorists claim over 50 identified genders, the seven main ones are Female, Male, Intersex, Trans, Non-Conforming, Personal, and Eunuch. It all depends on who you ask, but if you believe in the importance of these labels, it becomes obvious that the term gender has no single definition.

The correct term for gender theory is gender studies. This began as the academic study of women's interests, feminism, gender and politics. It then morphed into queer and men's studies in the 90's. This occurred during a social period best known as deconstruction. The philosophy of deconstruction is a loose set of views that text or words have no direct or true meaning that everyone sees the same. Yes, language is fluid and definitions do change over time, but deconstruction devalues descriptive language at its core. Gender no longer means what it once did and if some had their way, the terms man and woman would also cease to be definitive. The opposite of deconstruction is reconstruction which we see exhibited in the new labels and catch phrases such as trans women are women. Control the language and you control the narrative.

This is all semantics, the control of language. While everyone is distracted by terminology, definitions, and debate, the main subject has been evident without the need for words. A cat cannot be a dog, a tree become a flower, an anatomically correct human cannot become the opposite sex. No written or spoken word can make this happen. No matter what words or argument you use this reality does not change, it is scientifically impossible to change your sex. There are millions of Americans that say otherwise. This is their belief or faith in an alternate reality that they prefer to accept. You can't expect or demand everyone else to share it. This is just another faith-based group like hundreds of others that include religions. The Christians don't demand you call them brother or sister while using thee, thine and thou pronouns. Wouldn't that be annoying? Maybe understanding the comparison could make progressives understand what they're asking for. This could lead to true enlightenment. This is the trans manual's last observation on the matter.

Author's Note

This book is the culmination of years of observation. Since I could remember my parents often said they wanted a girl and instead they got me. Their disappointment did not go unnoticed. This did not make me wish to be a girl, but I did feel like an unwanted burden growing up. I watched as other kids were affected by their parents' words, and made sure I never did the same to my child. I saw my brother-in-law tell his son as a toddler that he was an accident and that he was unwanted. Then watched its long-term effects over twenty years.

When I was 11 in the early 70's it seemed as if everyone my age had long hair accept me. My parents viewed it as unhygienic. This desire to be like everyone else made me physically ill with suicidal thoughts which I never told anyone about. Fortunately, they relented to a styled cut. So yes, I know how it feels to be dysphoric over an obsession.

I realized then as I do now that my misery was caused by an obsession, it was not innate. I've talked with teens in detention centers, in the streets, raised a daughter, granddaughter and a few girlfriends' kids for a number of years. All with positive results. This book is my way of sharing my experience, views, and observations over the decades. My intent is that it brings some good into the world. My hope is that it relieves some suffering.

www.ingramcontent.com/pod-product-compliance
Lightning Source LLC
Chambersburg PA
CBHW051517030726

47592CB00006B/2314